The Journey Just Begun...
Thanks For Your Input =.

Kyle

Praise for *The Culture*

"Great message and inspirational! *The Culture* is a powerful reminder of what effective leadership is all about. It provides a road map for the journey toward organizational excellence."

— Bill Simpson
President & CEO, *Hershey Entertainment & Resorts Company*

"Great, great read. Jim's first two books remain a treasure for our company and no different for his third. You did it again, Jim. A true grand slam!"

— Dave Skogen
Chairman, *Festival Foods*

"From my professional military career to my 20-year marriage and the relationship with my children, *The Culture* "lights a fire in my gut" - Destined to be another best-seller from Jim Hunter!"

— Christopher R. Stricklin
Colonel, *United States Air Force*

"A great book about how to create a culture of excellence to drive business performance and competitive advantage. Don't miss the opportunity to become your best!"

— John Vella
Senior Vice President, *Nestlé Purina PetCare*

"Jim has produced a wonderfully colorful and substantive follow-up book that really hits at what his Servant Leadership system does best—making his teachings stick and become habits. A must-read for anyone serious about creating a culture that will endure and excel."

— Stephen Kircher
President, *Boyne Resorts*

"In this sequel to *The Servant*, Jim essentially pulls the human values we can all feel in The Golden Rule and assembles them into a convincing leadership development program."

— Tim Edens
Brigadier General, *United States Army*

"I have personally experienced in two organizations and in countless individuals the life-changing power of the principles Jim presents in this engaging sequel to *The Servant*. I encourage you to do the same if you aspire to the huge competitive advantage these principles provide."

— Gary S. Smith, Sr.
President & CEO, *Kentucky Trailer* (A Servant Leader Company)

"Jim has gone to great lengths to provide us with the roadmap to be "the first among equals" by being the best we are capable of while leading others to do the same."

— Jim Lynch, Ed. D.
Superintendent of Schools, East Greenwich, New Jersey

"Servant Leadership is the key to creating and sustaining a high-performing team and culture leading to performance excellence. James Hunter's writings have inspired our leadership team to serve."

— David Tilton
President & CEO, *AtlantiCare* (2009 Baldrige National Quality Award)

"I loved it! Jim's story is a powerful reminder that embedding servant leadership principles and practices deep into our organization is an ongoing, lifelong, commitment."

— Jim Gordon
Vice Chairman of the Board, *Gordon Food Service*

"Jim Hunter has done it again! *The Culture* is a short and refreshing story that illustrates how to effectively build and lead high-performing teams. For anyone looking to improve their impact as a leader, this is an inspiring read."

— Joseph M. DePinto
President & CEO, *7-Eleven, Inc.* (West Point Class of 1986)

"This is a home run, Jim's best book yet! We have been utilizing the Servant Leadership principles Jim presents in his books for over 15 years, and they have been the cornerstone that has allowed us to have been named a Baldrige National Quality Award recipient three times. Jim's latest book, *The Culture*, is a wealth of instruction on how to be a Servant Leader and to implement the principles."

— John Heer (Three-Time Baldrige National Quality Award recipient)
CEO (former), *North Mississippi Health Services & Baptist Hospital (Pensacola)*

"Since being introduced to Jim's servant leadership over ten years ago, teams I've been humbled to be a part of actively incorporate these principles with tremendous team-building results and mission success. *The Culture* is a MUST READ for all leaders who are "green and growing" and desire to up their game as a servant leader."
— Barre R. Seguin
Major General, *United States Air Force*

"A masterpiece on Servant Leadership. A must-read for anyone in a leadership position!"
— Garry L. Thompson,
Colonel, *United States Army*

"Hunter teaches us that truly excellent organizations always possess two things: great leadership and great culture. This book is a wonderful roadmap for building excellence"
— Stephen J. Szilagyi
Supply Chain Executive, *Lowe's Companies, Inc.*

"If you are looking for a catalyst to take your leadership to the next level, you absolutely need to read *The Culture!* This book will inspire you to make a difference and significantly change your life."
— Mark R. Pimpo
Captain, SC, *United States Navy*

(The views expressed are my own and do not reflect the official policy or position of the United States Navy, Department of Defense, or the U. S. Government.)

"Like Jim's other books, I really enjoyed this one - the simple blocking and tackling basics. Too often, businesses want a magic pill that is "different" - If we can build off this foundational message, we will always be green and growing. We are excited to share this book with our team!"
— Mark Skogen
CEO & President, *Festival Foods*

"Reading *The Culture* was a reminder of why culture and leadership are so important and yet so difficult to develop. Fortunately, this book provides an excellent roadmap for getting there."
— James Moore
CEO, *Atlantic Power Corporation*

ALSO BY JAMES C. HUNTER

The Servant

The World's Most Powerful Leadership Principle

THE CULTURE

CREATING EXCELLENCE WITH THOSE YOU LEAD

BY GROWING LEADERS & BUILDING COMMUNITY

JAMES C. HUNTER

This is a work of fiction. Names, characters, places, and incidents either are the product of the author's imagination or are used fictitiously. Any resemblance to actual persons, living or dead, events, or locales is entirely coincidental.

Copyright © 2017 by James C. Hunter

ALL RIGHTS RESERVED. This book contains material protected under International and Federal Copyright Laws and Treaties. Any unauthorized reprint or use of this material is prohibited. No part of this book may be reproduced or transmitted in any form or by any means, electronic or mechanical, including photocopying, recording, or by any information storage and retrieval system without express written permission from the author/publisher.

Available at special discounts for bulk purchases. For more information, visit www.jameshunter.com.

Cover and interior design by JETLAUNCH.net

Published by JDH
Grosse Ile, MI

ISBN: 978-1-944878-55-9

Printed in the United States of America

10 9 8 7 6 5 4 3 2

*To the One who makes
everything possible.*

Contents

Chapter One: Failure 1

Chapter Two: Return 7

Chapter Three: Reunion 13

Chapter Four: Culture 19

Chapter Five: Responsibility 27

Chapter Six: Skill 33

Chapter Seven: Power 41

Chapter Eight: Authority 49

Chapter Nine: Serving 55

Chapter Ten: Coaching 63

Chapter Eleven: More Coaching 71

Chapter Twelve: Character 79

Chapter Thirteen: Chaos 87

Chapter Fourteen: The Gift 93

Chapter Fifteen: Environment 99

Chapter Sixteen: Faking 107

Chapter Seventeen: Fighting 113

Chapter Eighteen: Forming 121

Chapter Nineteen: Functioning 129

Chapter Twenty: Growing Leaders 137

Chapter Twenty-One: Building Community 145

Chapter Twenty-Two: Execution 155

Afterword 163

Appendix A: Personal Barriers to Community 165

Appendix B: Leadership Skills Inventory 167

Appendix C: "Culture-Building Session" - Agenda 169

Appendix D: "Culture Building Session" - Guidelines 171

Appendix E: Coaching 173

Appendix F: Growing Leaders 175

Appendix G: Building Community 177

About the Author 179

Acknowledgments 180

THE
CULTURE

Chapter One

FAILURE

*Failure is not the falling down
But the staying down.*

Mary Pickford

What a loser.
 Better than two years had passed since my weeklong retreat to St. John of the Cross.[1]

After completing the retreat, I was excited and optimistic about what I had learned, certain my life would radically change for the better.

Things turned out just as I had hoped.

Only different.

My life was once again spiraling out of control. Even

---

1   An old Benedictine monastery located in the northwest corner of Michigan's lower peninsula. My experiences there are recounted in my first book, *The Servant: A Simple Story About the True Essence of Leadership*.

The Culture

my recurring nightmare from childhood had returned to haunt me.[2]

After returning home following that remarkable week at the monastery, I was certain of two things: 1) I had 'found' Simeon and had truly "listened" to him, and 2) I would soon be settling into a new and transformed life.

I whiffed on both.

For the two years following the retreat, the sergeant faithfully emailed the retreat participants with information regarding possible reunion dates.

The participants, or Gang of Seven (as the sergeant called us), included the coach, the nurse, the preacher, the principal, the sergeant, the teacher, and, of course, me, the manager.

Initially, our plan was to return to the monastery for a reunion six months after that incredible week. No one imagined it would take better than two years before we would gather again.

The problem centered around the abbot (the head honcho at the monastery), who apparently had to give final approval before anything happened. The sergeant's emails revealed that Simeon (the teacher) had been unable to obtain permission from the abbot for the reunion, which

---

[2] As told in *The Servant*: "I am lost and running for my very life through a cemetery on a moonless night. Though I cannot see what is chasing me, I *know* it to be evil, desiring me great harm. Suddenly, a figure covered head to toe in a black-hooded robe steps out from behind a large, crumbling concrete crucifix, and I crash directly into him (it). This primordial faceless being grabs my shoulders and urgently shouts, "Find Simeon! Find Simeon and listen to him!",." At which point I would awaken, shaking, drenched in a cold sweat."

Chapter One: Failure

irritated me to no end. (I had met the old geezer during the retreat, and let's just say I was not impressed.)

Simeon needed permission? Really? Simeon (his monastic given name) was the former Len Hoffman. The Len Hoffman, who prior to entering the monastery was a corporate legend, one of the most successful CEOs in American history. This great man needed 'permission' from the old abbot for a little friendly get together?

Give me a break.

After what I assume were months of ring-kissing and groveling, Simeon prevailed. In his infinite wisdom and divine leniency, the abbot finally granted a special dispensation for us to meet.

Apparently, the monastery would be deserted while Simeon's thirty-two fellow monks attended a worldwide Benedictine conference in Rome. Simeon had received special permission to remain behind to watch over the monastery, as well as host a weekend reunion with the Gang of Seven.

I made a mental note to send the abbot a thank-you letter and gift for his immeasurable kindnesses and mercies.

Or not.

As you probably noticed, my attitude was pretty far south of where it needed to be as the reunion weekend approached.

Full disclosure: I was dreading the reunion.

I felt like a complete failure for not following through on all the great leadership lessons I had learned two years prior. I was flat-out embarrassed to reconnect with my

3

classmates, not having my act together. And worst of all, I was mortified to face Simeon and experience what I was certain would be his great disappointment in me.

Mind you, looking from the outside in, it appeared that I had the world by the tail, and I worked hard to promote that impression. Big job, large home, beautiful wife, two kids in high school, recreational toys, regular vacations in warm places—I was living large, baby. The American dream.

You're playing way above the rim, bro', was how my sports-fanatic brother-in-law described me.

Little did he know, things are often not as they appear.

Oh, I started out strong in the early weeks following the retreat. My family, friends, and coworkers frequently commented on the wonderful transformation they were observing in me.

But it didn't last.

Slowly, inexorably, former patterns of obsessive control and manipulation (some would say abusive) behaviors resurfaced, along with a few other nasty behaviors.

My relationship with my wife, Rachael, had seriously deteriorated, and we were entertaining a trial separation. If not for our two kiddos, I am certain we would have already called it quits.

My sixteen-year-old, John Jr., had gone from being loud and rebellious two years prior, to being an extreme introvert, spending untold hours in his room playing raunchy video games or surfing online on God-only-knows-what websites. His grades at school were barely passing, and his only friend was one very strange dude. In short, my son was starting to scare me a little. Actually, more than a little.

And then there was my little girl, Sarah. I still tear up reflecting upon our unique daddy/daughter relationship before her teen years. Now fourteen, she was

Chapter One: Failure

hanging with a group of girls who dressed in black while swearing off makeup and boys. I had recently uncovered some other disturbing stuff I can't even bring myself to mention.

Our once-special relationship had been reduced to one-syllable words (hi, bye, fine, not! sucks). The last time she actually engaged me in conversation was when she announced her decision to have a large dragon tattoo etched above her rear-end, which supposedly represented strength, courage, or some other nonsense.

"No daughter of mine is getting a 'tramp stamp' on my watch," I declared, slamming my fist on the dinner table for dictatorial emphasis.

"Whatever," was her only response, although between us I was pleased to hear her utter a three-syllable word.

Within a week, she was strutting around the house with the dragon on open display along with a nose ring thrown in to dramatize whatever point she was trying to make. The month grounding she received made her even more defiant and distant.

Dark clouds were also forming at work, my usual safe haven, with ominous rumors of employee unrest and another unionization attempt in my plant. A peer plant manager from a sister factory had given me a heads-up that corporate was not happy with my performance. The rumor was that some paper-pushing HR rep had labeled me 'emotionally immature.' Really? What did they know about running a multi-million-dollar manufacturing operation?

To ice the cake, two weeks prior to the reunion, my boss put me on a PIP (performance improvement plan), which essentially meant I had 120 days to get my act together or else they would be looking for a new general manager at the glass factory.

The Culture

As I set out for our reunion that sunny Friday afternoon in October for the six-hour drive to northern Michigan, I simply could not believe the current state of my life.
What a loser.

Chapter Two

RETURN

*Courage is being scared to death...
and saddling up anyway.*

John Wayne

Despite my depressed state, the view outside my windshield cheered me considerably.

For me, the northwest corner of Michigan's lower peninsula is one of the most lovely and picturesque places in the world, especially in autumn.

My SUV sped along scenic highway M-22, past the lovely town of Frankfort, before crossing 'the narrows' bridge, which divides 'little' and 'big' Glen Lake, one of the most beautiful freshwater lakes on the planet. To my left and above the western shore of little Glen, I caught a glimpse of the golden sun setting behind the monstrous sand dune known as Dune Climb, a popular tourist challenge I had often conquered as a kid.

A few minutes later, I came to the charming town of

Glen Arbor and parked at the corner eatery known as Boone Docks where I listened to live music while wolfing down a scrumptious burger. From there, I walked over to Cherry Republic to pick up a sack of chocolate-covered cherries for Rachael (her favorite), before moseying down to Art's Tavern for a cup of coffee and a piece of their famous cobbler à la mode.

Back on the road, I drove a few miles past The Homestead Freshwater Resort before turning north onto the dirt road leading to Pyramid Point. It was now dark, so I crept along slowly for a couple of miles, looking for the hard-to-find two-track trail leading back to the monastery.

I nearly missed the solitary fence pole that was off the road to my left. Fastened to the pole was a simple wooden board with the carved letters: St. John of the Cross.

I was back.

Upon exiting my vehicle, I was immediately gripped by the darkness and solitude of my surroundings. I paused to listen to the dry, rustling autumn leaves combined with the roar of the Lake Michigan surf crashing in the dark far below. These lovely sounds brought immediate comfort to my troubled soul.

I grabbed my backpack and made my way over to the guest house. The registration area was vacant but there was a note taped to the desktop:

Chapter Two: Return

> *Greetings, My Friend:*
> *I am looking forward to our time together . . . You will have your own room this weekend (I know you prefer rooming alone) – #2 upstairs.*
> *We are starting at 8am sharp in the main lodge – Same room as last time.*
> *I love you, John.*
> *† Simeon*

My first feeling was elation over not having to share a room with anyone. How thoughtful of Simeon to remember.

My second was discomfort over the "I love you" part of the teacher's note. Those three words had never set well with me coming from a man.

As I unpacked, I noticed my dark mood lifting and being replaced by something I had not felt in some time. It was the same feeling I had experienced sitting in the parking lot waiting for Rachael to pick me up following the retreat, twenty-six months earlier.

Hope.

Maybe this time I would 'find Simeon and listen to him.'

Really listen to him.

Hope must be a good thing because I slept better than I had in a long time.

As is my custom, I rose early, dressed quickly, and made my way outside. Dawn was evident on the far horizon, and a chilly westerly breeze was blowing in off the barely visible great lake.

I walked to the edge of the giant sand cliff and stood near the staircase leading down to the beach. I turned to take in the beautiful surroundings, pleased that it was as I remembered.

The monastery was nestled in magnificent sand dunes, several hundred feet above Lake Michigan. A half-dozen small and medium-sized log buildings surrounded the chapel, a hexagonal structure that was the focal point of the campus.

The aged wooden chapel's six walls converged to the center to form the steeple with a large cross affixed at its apex. Beautiful, intricate stained glass depicting biblical stories were on each of the six sides. Simple, but elegant.

I turned back toward the immense lake, and in the twilight, I detected movement in the water just off the beach. It appeared to be someone strolling in the morning surf.

My heart skipped a beat.

Could it be him?

I quickly but carefully made my way down the old staircase, navigating around many broken steps. Once on flat sand, I surprised myself by actually running toward the figure strolling in the water.

"Simeon," I yelled over the noise of the surf, not caring as I waded up to my thighs in the freezing water, "Is that you?"

The figure in the black hooded gown turned slowly before greeting me with a long and warm embrace. I had to reach up a little to hug Simeon as he was three or four inches taller than my six-foot frame.

I had forgotten the impact of being in the teacher's presence. Simeon had not visibly aged and still appeared in excellent condition. His deeply-tanned face bore chiseled cheekbones, rugged lines, and a prominent chin and nose. He had snow-white hair. He looked to be in his sixties rather than his actual eighty-four years of age.

As before, what struck me most were his penetrating, steely blue eyes. They were absolutely the most accepting, loving, non-judgmental eyes I had ever experienced. Being in his presence was disarming, giving me a feeling of complete emotional and psychic safety.

"How is my good friend?" he asked, before hugging me again.

Suddenly and unexpectedly an extremely rare event occurred.

I began to cry.

I tried to respond to the question but could not get out a lucid word. Simeon put his arm tightly around my shoulder before we waded to shore and made our way back up the 243 steps to the top of the sand dune.

As we sat on a bench overlooking the lake, you would have thought I had run a marathon by the way I was huffing and puffing from the climb. The teacher was not winded in the least.

We sat for some time before the words began to come.

"Simeon, I feel like such a failure! The retreat two years ago was the highlight of my life, and I was so sure I would totally change for the better. Things were great for the first few months, but now it's worse than ever."

The teacher did not ask a question or make a single comment. He only sat looking intently into my eyes taking in my every word, as if nothing mattered except this particular moment in space and time.

"Why didn't I change, Simeon?" I pleaded. "I believed everything we were taught about leadership, serving others, and building relationships. Yet, as you can see, I'm still a mess."

The teacher looked at me with total compassion and complete acceptance. His smile and gaze were so penetrating and disarming that I found it difficult to maintain eye contact.

"You're not saying anything, Simeon," I blurted out, a little annoyed by his silence. "What are you thinking?"

"I am so happy you are here, John."

Chapter Three

REUNION

*There is no value in learning well
if you neglect to do well.*

Third-Grade School Teacher

We sat on the bench in silence, taking in the splendor. Above the enormous blue lake, the orange-red morning sky was creating a kaleidoscope of colors of immense beauty. I could feel the stress knots coming out of my life rope.

After some time had passed, Simeon whispered, "It's time to go."

Still not wanting to face my classmates or the weekend ahead, I halfheartedly followed the teacher to the main lodge and entered the meeting room where we had met for our retreat two years prior.

The lovely room was as I remembered, inviting and comfortable with wall-to-wall carpeting, ornate bookshelves, along with beautifully accented woodwork

The Culture

throughout the room, all handcrafted by what must have been highly-skilled people. The seating consisted of two old but comfy couches, one recliner/rocker, along with several high-backed wooden chairs (thankfully padded) scattered about.

The room's west wall had several large windows facing Lake Michigan, each perfectly framing and capturing the spectacular view. Centered on the north wall was a massive natural stone fireplace, obviously created by talented masons. The teacher wasted no time building a fire with the kindling and white birch handily available, which quickly took the morning chill out of the room. In the northwest corner stood a very old, ornate grandfather clock that began to chime, informing us it was half past the hour.

Over the next thirty minutes, the remaining five from our Gang of Seven rolled in, and the room was soon buzzing with excitement and hugging. I was never much of the hugging type, yet I was enthusiastically in the middle of it all, temporarily placing my insecurities and other issues on hold. It was as though the group had never been apart.

Before long, the old clock chimed the first of eight bells.

Remembering the teacher was a stickler about time, we hustled to grab a seat.

To begin, the teacher suggested we each weigh in by sharing a personal update of our lives including highlights and lowlights of the past two years.

Simeon went first, and I was touched by how deeply and personally he shared. He talked openly about his joys, frustrations, accomplishments, failures, and spiritual struggles with complete transparency, vulnerability, and candor.

When finished, the teacher scanned the room and

Chapter Three: Reunion

invited my roommate from our first retreat, Lee (the preacher), to share next. Surprisingly, the preacher grunted something unintelligible and even appeared irritated at being chosen. He then proceeded to detail some basic, superficial information as though he were answering an oral questionnaire from the DMV. He seemed different from the guy I knew before.

Disappointingly, the rest of the group chose to follow the preacher's shallow example rather than the teacher's inspiring one.

Theresa (the principal) told us she had transferred to a large inner-city public high school district in Detroit while Kim (the nurse) said she continued to practice nursing at Providence Hospital, also downstate. Chris (the coach) stated she was now the women's head basketball coach at a large state university and proudly announced her team had made it to the NCAA Women's Final Four the previous spring, causing the group to break into applause. Greg (the sergeant), with military-like precision, told us of his recent promotion to platoon sergeant at Fort Campbell, Kentucky, where he led combat veterans returning from Iraq or Afghanistan, many who had endured multiple tours of duty. This brought another round of applause.

When the sergeant finished, all eyes settled in on me. I felt the blood rising to my face and neck as the room started spinning. My eyes filled with tears as I lowered my head, unable to speak.

"Cat got your tongue, boy?" the preacher jabbed.

Someone sat down next to me on the couch, and, since I was staring at the floor, I quickly deduced the highly polished black shoes belonged to the sergeant. He put his arm around my shoulder, which only served to increase the flow of tears.

A true horror show was unfolding as I broke down

in front of everyone. I firmly pinched my forearm, vainly attempting to awaken myself from what I was sure was a bad dream.

After what seemed an eternity, but was probably less than a minute, the coach humanely got the attention off me by inquiring about the agenda for the weekend.

"I have been wondering the same thing, Chris," the teacher replied. "What would our little community like to accomplish this weekend?"

"You tell us; it's your show," the preacher snapped back, trying but failing to sound cute.

Ignoring his rudeness, I spontaneously blurted out, "I feel like a failure. I spent an entire week here with you people, learned some amazing lessons about leadership and life, only to return home and fall right back into my old ways. I'm ashamed to say I'm in worse shape now than I was two years ago. And as you all know, it was pretty bad then."

I couldn't believe those words came out of my mouth.

"Thank you for sharing that," the teacher immediately responded. "Such openness and honesty. I'm proud of you, John."

He continued. "And I suspect John is not the only one who has struggled. Two years ago, we spent much time discussing leadership, and you all left excited about the principles and eager to make changes.

"Yet how many of you can honestly say you have made significant and sustainable changes in your lives because of our time together?"

Expecting all hands to rise except mine, I was stunned as I surveyed the room.

Chapter Three: Reunion

Only one hand was raised, and that lone hand was attached to the man with the shiny black shoes.

I was not the only loser.

The preacher was incredulous.

"Do you mean to tell me the only one who had real and sustainable change is Greg? As I remember it, our friend the sergeant was the most combative and cynical one of all."

"That's right," I reacted, no longer able to hide my irritation. "But the difference between you and Greg is that he must have gone back and put what he learned into action. You're probably still praying about it!"

Where did that venom come from? I even surprised myself, but I took another shot anyway.

"Remember, Lee? Intentions minus actions equals squat. Or have you forgotten that lesson?"

The preacher's return volley was swift and cutting. "What's your problem, big guy? I thought you would feel better after your little cry."

I had no comeback.

Our happy little reunion was off to a rough start.

After a lengthy and awkward silence, the nurse rescued us from our discomfort.

"Why didn't we all change, Simeon? To be honest, I dreaded coming back here and facing you all. I was ashamed for not changing like I thought I would."

Kim's words were music to my ears and brought comfort to my aching heart.

And to think I had nearly wimped out and stayed home.

The nurse continued. "May I make a suggestion for our weekend? First, I need to understand why Greg was the only one who actually changed. Second, I want to know precisely how to go about making real and sustainable changes in my life. How do I move from learning about leadership to actually becoming an effective leader?"

The principal agreed. "I like it, Kim. I would also like to pick Simeon's brain about how to create a great culture and build a high-performing leadership team. To be honest, my high school staff is pretty dysfunctional, and I feel responsible."

Beginning to feel excited, I added, "If your definition of culture and team includes business, family, and marital issues, I'm all in. I need all the help I can get!"

Did I just say that?

Around the room, many heads were nodding.

Carefully taking it all in, the teacher summed up.

"Okay, here's what I'm hearing. Our Gang of Seven will define and explore the steps to sustainable change and creating a culture of excellence. A place where leadership, excellence, high-performance teamwork, community, and continuous improvement can thrive at work, home, school, the ball field, or wherever we choose to lead.

"We only have two days together, so we will need to be efficient. Today, let's dig into defining culture and leadership. Tomorrow, we'll explore the steps necessary to creating a culture of excellence by growing leaders and building community."

"Is everyone in?"

Heads were enthusiastically bobbing up and down.

Every head but the preacher's.

Chapter Four

CULTURE

Culture eats strategy for breakfast.

Peter Drucker

The coach was pumped. "Simeon, I can't think of a better person to lead us on our journey this weekend! Especially considering that in your day you led some of the highest-performing organizations in America. I can't wait to start uploading some of your wisdom."

I'm pretty sure the teacher blushed. "So kind of you to say, Chris."

The sergeant was curious. "Simeon, looking back on your distinguished career, what was your biggest takeaway about leadership?"

There was no hesitation. "That's an easy one, Greg. The essential task of the leader is to create and sustain an environment or culture of excellence wherever they lead. To

The Culture

this day, I am haunted by my missed opportunities before I understood the power of culture in any organization.

"Perhaps some of you remember reading about Lou Gerstner, who took over as CEO at IBM during a particularly vulnerable time in its history. He was credited with leading that prestigious but floundering organization through an amazing transformation.

"Mr. Gerstner was fond of saying that the main thing he learned at IBM was that culture is everything. I became a true believer in this principle as well."

The principal was frowning. "I hate to be a stick in the mud, but can we please attach definitions to these words, so we all know what we're talking about? My years in education have taught me that defining our terms is essential to learning. When you use the word 'culture,' what exactly are you referring to?"

The teacher smiled. "Thank you, and you are correct, Theresa. Words are important, and clarity is our friend."

"Simeon," the coach waded in, "may I take a stab at defining culture? Not long ago, I completed a coach's workshop on culture, and I learned a ton."

"By all means, Chris."

"Culture is the way a group goes about its business and gets things done. If personal character is how a person behaves when no one is looking, a group's culture is the collective character or behavior of its members.

"This includes the group's values, beliefs, attitudes, and practices which lay the foundation for how team members behave, interact, and connect. An organization's culture—or, more precisely, the way it behaves—creates dynamics and synergies ranging from highly performing to highly dysfunctional."

The teacher was impressed. "Bravo, Chris, you did learn a ton. And you captured the true essence of culture by stating it is how people actually behave. Who then is the key person in determining the culture of a group?"

"That would be the individual group leader," the coach matter-of-factly stated. "The university website where I work advertises our culture of excellence, but that is simply not true. We have pockets of excellence, but what really matters is who is in charge of the pocket. There are departments where the leader tolerates mediocrity, and that is exactly what they get. Conversely, the chair of my department is always pushing us toward excellence, and that is precisely what she gets."

"She gets what she expects," the principal concurred. "There is an old saying in classroom management that everyone who enters the room has two basic questions. Question one, how am I supposed to behave? Question two, what happens if I don't? Every day, the leader and the culture provide answers and reinforcements to those two questions."

The sergeant agreed. "Thank you for that, ma'am, and I think you're dead on. My experience is that culture is a powerful driver of behavior, and the group leader sets the tone. A great culture produces excellence, while mediocrity breeds the same. I witness it daily in our military."

"So, is culture like the organization's mission statement?" the nurse asked.

The teacher clarified. "Culture goes much deeper than a mission statement, Kim. Culture is not what we think, or say, or advertise, or even believe about the organization. Culture is how group members actually behave, repeatedly and habitually.

"There are many examples of well-known organizations that crashed and burned following scandalous behavior. These organizations often had beautiful mission statements

The Culture

and lofty core values etched in marble on the walls of their corporate headquarters. Unfortunately, their words were not aligned with their actions."

The sergeant was nodding. "That is correct, sir. People get their behavioral cues, not by what some poster says, but by what actually goes on in an organization day in and day out. What behaviors get you recognized and rewarded? What behaviors are frowned upon and get you in hot water? Through observation and repeated practice, habitual group behaviors are formed that over time becomes the group's culture."

The teacher was emphatic. "Simply put, culture is an organization's competitive advantage. We are living in a world of global competition and commoditization where products, services, technologies, and even key people can be bought, pirated, or recruited by competitors. Nearly every organization must compete head to head with little product or technological differentiation or advantage."

"And your point?" the preacher mumbled, sounding bored, which made me cringe.

The teacher was undeterred. "The point, Lee, is that an organization's competitive advantage lies in creating a culture that can deliver excellence to its stakeholders and sustain it over time. A place that attracts great people in the form of customers, employees, shareholders, and vendors. That is why great leaders are laser-focused on creating and sustaining a culture of excellence—because they know if they build it, people will come."

The nurse seemed intrigued. "I think I am getting it, but I'm more of a visual learner. Simeon, could you create a mind picture or metaphor for me of what this culture thing looks like so I can better get my head around it?"

The teacher paused. "Let's try this, Kim. Think of a great culture like a majestic bald eagle. The eagle has the

Chapter Four: Culture

distinct competitive advantage of soaring high above its enemies as well as its prey because of the bird's huge and powerful wings.

"Now picture one wing representing great leadership and the other wing great teamwork or community. When both wings are functioning well together, the eagle gets a lot further, a lot faster. A huge competitive advantage."

The nurse struggled for clarity. "Okay, let me be sure I've got this culture thing. An organization is simply two or more people gathered for a purpose, so these principles apply to any group. Over time, as group members interact and perform, expectations and standards of normative behavior emerge and are reinforced daily. These behaviors become the group's collective habits, which becomes the culture. Is that the general idea?"

"That's the essence of it, Kim," the teacher replied. "And here's another metaphor for you. Culture is like the tide in the harbor where the boats rise if expectations and behaviors are high and fall if expectations and behaviors are low. Establishing and sustaining a culture of excellence involves creating the necessary conditions to keep the tide in the harbor as high as possible."

"Exactly!" the sergeant reacted excitedly. "A great culture defines, teaches, demands, and rewards excellence. And when excellence becomes the standard, the group begins to monitor and police itself to ensure that the new normal—the culture—is sustained.

"Here's another mind picture for you, Kim. A great culture is like antibodies in our blood stream which continually monitor our bodies to protect and defend it against threats. When they encounter dangers, they zero in to destroy the threat to ensure our optimal health. This is the potential power of culture within an organization."

The teacher nodded. "To reiterate, you create a culture

of excellence by getting laser focused on the two wings of the eagle, growing leaders and building community."

"Growing leaders, building community. Define your terms, please," the principal reminded.

Simeon laughed. "Thank you, Theresa. By growing leaders, I am referring to the process of assisting people in developing their leadership skills, specifically their character, which is the essential foundation of leadership. We will explore this in detail later today.

"And by building community or high-performing teams, I am referring to the process of building trust and improving the way the group connects and works together. Synonyms for community include teamwork, esprit de corps, camaraderie, and togetherness. Its essence is creating a psychologically safe place where group members support and encourage one another, resolve conflict rather than avoid it, and take personal responsibility for the success of the team."

The preacher wasn't buying it. "I'm not seeing what the big deal is here, how this nebulous thing called culture actually drives the performance and behavior of people. Got some examples?"

"Been to your local DMV lately, Lee?" I sarcastically threw back at him. "If the people working there moved any slower, I think their hearts would stop beating. Unfortunately, the public has come to expect it from many governmental agencies."

"Or have you read about the recent emissions debacle at VW?" the principal offered. "They actually created software to give false readings to pass government emission standards. Early indications point to a toxic culture of fear and intimidation that led to an elaborate deception and cover up. They're saying it's going to cost VW tens of billions of dollars before it's over."

The sergeant added, "In our NCO leadership training, we analyzed Korean Airlines, who had a deplorable safety record and was the laughing stock of the industry two decades ago. They brought in an outsider to fix it and discovered the culprit was a culture of rigid hierarchy including never questioning a superior. In the cockpit, that culture proved disastrous when junior crew members refused to challenge senior crew members' decisions even as they flew the jet right into the side of a mountain. Once they changed the culture, the safety problems subsided.

"On the flip side, Southwest Airlines is known for their culture of excellence, where flight attendants operate as a team of all leaders taking personal responsibility for their airplane. Their values include a warrior mentality, a servant spirit, and having fun. And that's how they behave. They really believe that stuff at Southwest."

The coach shared her story. "Not long ago, my husband was diagnosed with prostate cancer, and we sought treatment at the Cancer Treatment Centers of America. We have never experienced such a high level of service and care, a true culture of excellence. It was like everyone in the place operated according to the principle, 'The answer is yes, now what is your question?'

"It didn't matter what you needed, even a hotel issue or trouble with your car. They told us our job was to get well, and their job was to take care of everything else. And that's exactly how they behaved across the board."

The teacher summed up. "Now the good news is that we have the know-how of how to create a culture of excellence through growing leaders and building community. Indeed, the know-how has been around for centuries.

"The bad news is that excellence requires great commitment and effort. Unfortunately, many are not up to the challenge and settle for less."

I must admit my skepticism meter was spiking in the red zone. Culture? Growing leaders? Building community? I wasn't seeing the connection between these things and my utter failures as a boss, husband, and father.

Then again, based on my track record, who was I to judge or discount anything being said?

'Find Simeon and listen to him.'

The time had come.

Chapter Five

RESPONSIBILITY

*Leadership is serious meddling
in other people's lives.*

Max DePree

The teacher moved us forward.

"Now that we have defined culture, let's move on to what makes a culture excellent, namely great leadership and strong community.

"Let's begin with leadership. Does anyone remember our working definition of leadership from two years ago?"

"Let me find it," the principal responded as she scrolled through her phone.

Simeon moved to the north end of the room by the large whiteboards. As Theresa read, he wrote:

Leadership = The skill of influencing people to enthusiastically work toward goals identified as being for the common good.

The Culture

"Thank you, Theresa. Using our definition as a springboard, I would like each of you to share with the group what you believe to be the single most important quality of leadership."

The nurse dove right in. "For me, I'm humbled by the huge responsibility of being in a position of leadership."

The teacher wrote it down:

Leadership = Awesome Responsibility

The principal snickered. "You all know I love quotes, so I'll hit you with another one. Peter Drucker used to say that leadership is not a rank, it is a responsibility."

"Indeed it is," the teacher concurred. "Back in my CEO days, I would regularly remind our leaders that their employees are stuck in the bowels of their ship for 50% of their waking hours. Most employees spend more waking hours at work than they do with their families. Leadership is an incredible responsibility."

The nurse added, "Or think about the role of leadership in marriage. I mean think about it—another human being commits to spending their life with you. What a staggering responsibility that goes along with that commitment."

"Or the responsibility of having children," the principal suggested. "If I'm your kid, I am stuck with you for the rest of my life. That fact will never change. You're it!"

The sergeant got serious. "And we signed up for these awesome responsibilities. No one forces us to be the boss, get married, have kids, or become a coach or a teacher. Leadership is a very high calling."

The coach added, "I was recently reading a book about the late, great UCLA basketball coach, John Wooden, who Sporting News called the best coach ever. He called

Chapter Five: Responsibility

leadership a sacred trust. Think of that. As leaders, human beings have been entrusted to our care for seasons of their lives. It's humbling to think about."

The preacher didn't seem to think so.

"Being a leader is a high calling? A sacred trust? Let's not get carried away here, folks. Missionaries, or people in the clergy, now that's a high calling, something sacred."

More than a couple of us rolled our eyes.

"I'm not sure that's true, sir," the sergeant firmly but respectfully countered. "I can sit in church for an hour a week and forget most of what was said by Monday morning. But as Simeon said, I'm stuck with my leader for half of my waking hours. Think of the impact the leader can have on people's lives! An impact of good or bad. How many of you have worked for a bad boss?"

All hands (except the preacher's) immediately shot toward the ceiling.

The sergeant continued. "Did that bad boss impact your life? You bet they did. Three years ago, I had a terrible commanding officer, and she nearly did me in. If you've ever worked for a bad boss, you know exactly what I'm talking about.

"Carried away, sir? I don't think so. I am convinced leadership is a high calling, a sacred trust as Mr. Wooden said."

The principal concurred. "I agree. I mean, let's face it. If I've got a lousy boss, I've got a lousy job. And young people today have a low tolerance for bad bosses. In fact, recent polls show nearly 70% of young people who quit their job do not quit the company. They quit their boss. These young people don't think anything of quitting their organization to go to work for a better company or a leader that 'gets it.'"

"What do you see at the college level, Chris?" I asked.

"These young people coming up now are different. Did any of you see that 60 Minutes segment recently about the millennial employees, those born after 1980? These young people have high expectations of their leaders, much more than my generation did.

"These young people have grown up skeptical of power people and don't hesitate to speak their minds. When someone tells them, 'Do it or else,' their reaction is, 'What planet are you from, pal?' I suppose the mediocre ones will hang around, but when the best and brightest conclude their leaders don't get it, they move on."

"And who can blame them?" the nurse asked. "Most people want to be in an environment where they are valued and can contribute to something important. They want to grow and improve."

The coach added, "In my first role as an assistant coach at the collegiate level, my coach and mentor always said that the test of a great coach is this: Have your players raised their game as a result of spending a few seasons with you? And she was not only referring to their athletic abilities. She was mainly referring to whether or not they had grown as human beings. Are they better people? Has their character grown because of your leadership?"

"I love that test," the sergeant said. "Are your people better when they leave than when they arrived? Are they raising their game? If you want to know how you're doing as a leader, just look at those you're leading, and you'll have your answer."

"Or in business," I sheepishly added, feeling hypocritical. "Are your employees getting promoted? Are they in demand by other departments or even with outside employers? Will they have a better career because they spent time with you?"

"Or in the family," the principal interjected. "When your

Chapter Five: Responsibility

children leave your home, will they be ready to take on this big, bad world? Will they be good parents, spouses, neighbors, citizens, employees, or whomever they're called to be?" The teacher looked excited. "Love the inputs! I am convinced that this is where leadership begins. The very best leaders often reflect upon and have internalized the awesome responsibility of leadership.

"The great leaders I have known do not lay awake at night thinking about their next pay raise or getting a corner office. What keeps them awake is concern over whether or not their people have everything they need to be successful. Do they have the tools, training, mission, margin, rules of the house, hugs, spanks, communication—everything they need to win? The great ones are not focused on their rights; they are focused on their responsibilities."

The sergeant summed up. "And our responsibility as leaders is to serve those entrusted to our care by identifying and meeting their legitimate needs to enable them to be the best they are capable of becoming."

As I listened, I was amazed at how different the sergeant seemed from two years ago.

I also reflected upon the leadership roles I had signed up for as boss, father, husband, son, friend, neighbor—and began to apply the test. Were people well served under my leadership? Did they leave better than when they arrived? Did they raise their game as a result of my influence? Will they be glad I was there?

My answers to the test served only to depress me.

The teacher gave us a thirty-minute break, so the coach, nurse, and I walked over to the monastery commons to grab some coffee and a snack.

"How do you like the session so far?" Kim asked no one in particular.

"So far so good," I quickly responded. "But Lee is really getting on my nerves."

"Yeah, I know what you mean," Chris agreed. He can really be annoying with his sniping comments. You would think he would know better, being a pastor and all."

"I'm surprised Simeon doesn't say something," I added. For someone who used to be such a great leader in the real world, I'm shocked he lets that crap go on."

The coach nodded.

I glanced over at Kim, who was staring down at her coffee and looking uncomfortable. Suddenly, she rose and excused herself from the table.

Chris asked, "Is everything okay, Kim?"

"I'm just feeling uncomfortable with this conversation, so I'm going back. I'll see you in class."

The coach looked my way. "What's up with, Kim?"

"Beats me," I replied, utterly clueless to our duplicitous behavior.

Chapter Six

SKILL

Leadership can and must be learned.

Peter Drucker

Following the break, the teacher wasted no time moving forward.

"Kim, thank you for that reminder about the awesome yet humbling responsibility of leadership. Who's next?"

The sergeant's hand shot up.

"Sir, two years ago we talked about leadership being a skill, and I was skeptical at the time. My paradigm had always been that either you are a leader or you are not. I now know differently."

The teacher wrote:

Leadership = Skill

Simeon turned towards the sergeant. "I'm curious, Greg. What convinced you that leadership is a skill rather than a natural, inborn ability?"

The Culture

The sergeant laughed. "Born leaders? Seriously? We know leadership is about inspiring and influencing people to action and to excellence. We know influence is built through serving and sacrificing for others, which requires personal character.

"I now understand leadership is character in action, and character is not some trait you are born with. Personal character is a skill that each of us must hone and develop, choice by choice. I have come to believe that personal character is by far the most important skill any human being develops in their life."

"Wow, well put, Greg," the coach marveled. "My hero, the late coach Vince Lombardi, often said leaders were not born, they were made. Your insight makes that clear to me now."

The nurse snickered. "I guess a born leader does sound kind of silly. I mean, have you ever been around a two-year-old? We all admire leaders who demonstrate patience, selflessness, accountability, gratitude, honesty, and respectfulness. Do these character skills describe any two-year-olds you know?"

The principal laughed. "Two-year-olds demonstrate our human nature in all its glory. Cute, little, narcissistic tyrants running around the house screaming, 'Me first!' to anyone who will listen."

"Cute in a two-year-old," the nurse reacted, "but rather ugly in a twenty, forty, or sixty-year-old. I've met far too many executives dressed in expensive suits, sitting in corner offices, who never grew up emotionally. It's still all about them."

The teacher added, "Effective leaders have learned to get over themselves, their terrible twos, and become other-focused. They have learned one of life's toughest lessons, which is to keep your eye on the ball, and you are not the ball. The ball is our people, serving them by meeting their legitimate needs."

The principal weighed in, "In the interests of clarity, I just looked up the word 'skill' on my phone, and it's defined as 'a learned or acquired ability.' If leadership is indeed a skill, the implication is that the skill of leadership is available to anyone."

"I think almost anyone," I suggested. "As you know, my wife is a psychologist, whom I affectionately refer to as 'the shrink.' I've heard her say growth in personal character and relationship-building skills is available to nearly everyone, provided you are not suffering from a character disorder or narcissistic personality, relatively rare in the general population. Obviously, if you can't navigate relationships, you won't be able to do leadership because leadership is all about people and relationships.

"I guess what I'm saying is, if leadership is a skill, a learned or acquired ability, it's available to the vast majority of people who possess basic intellectual and psychological abilities."

The sergeant declared, "Of course leadership is a skill that can be developed! If not, what's the point of taking leadership classes or growing or extending yourself to be the best you can be? I get to watch leaders grow every day in the military."

"I think that's right, Greg," I replied. "Once we accept the fact that leadership is a skill, a learned or acquired ability, we are now on the hook. What are we doing to improve or raise our game?

"I mean, how can we ask those entrusted to our care, our children, employees, students, athletes—whomever we lead—how can we ask them to be the best they can be if we're not willing to be the best we can be? Do our employees or family see us growing? Are we better leaders than last year? Do we really believe in continuous improvement, or are those words just a punch line?

"But listen to me preach. What a hypocrite. I can talk all about what leadership is, but executing leadership—not so much."

The nurse had an insight. "You mentioned continuous improvement, John, and most everyone says that they believe in continuous improvement. But it just dawned on me that we cannot improve unless we change. And change can be difficult."

"That is empirically true, Kim," the principal acknowledged. "We cannot improve unless we change. As Einstein said, insanity is continuing to do what you've always done and hoping for different results."

The sergeant was nodding. "Roger that. My granddaddy was a farmer, and he loved to say, 'You are either green and growing or ripe and rotting.' I think he was on to something because nothing living stays the same. I mean, even if you think you're the same as you were even a year ago, the world is changing and moving by you at such a high rate of speed that, by definition, you're going backward."

"Unfortunately," I pessimistically interjected, "my experience in the business world is that we don't really believe leadership is a skill at all. We don't really believe leadership is a learned or acquired ability."

The nurse looked confused. "Why would you say that, John?"

"Because the reality is this. When it's time to promote someone, we simply take our best task people and make them the leader.

"You've all seen it play out. We take the best forklift driver, and we make them the supervisor. Now we've lost our best forklift driver, and we've got a terrible supervisor. Or we take the best salesperson and make them the sales manager. Now we've lost our best salesperson, and we're

Chapter Six: Skill

stuck with a horrible leader."

The teacher smiled. "So true, John. Just because you can do the job well does not mean you can inspire and influence other people to do the job well. Leadership is a completely different skill set.

"I have met scores of managers, executives, military officers, and others who have read all the books and been to all the seminars about leadership but have never incorporated the skills of leadership into their life. The truth is, you can know all about leadership yet never know leadership."

"So true, Simeon!" the sergeant exclaimed. "My commander, and she's brilliant, calls this militant ignorance."

"Definition please?" the principal requested.

"I apologize, ma'am. My commander says that ignorance is what you don't know. Militant ignorance is what you think you know but don't know. And the militant ones are usually the most certain about what they don't know."

The principal launched another quote. "Mark Twain used to say, 'It ain't what you don't know that gets you into trouble. It's what you know for sure that just ain't so.'"

I laughed. "Amen, sister. I think this is also true in the mental health profession. My wife, the shrink, forces me every year to endure yet another Christmas party with her colleagues. I swear to you, I've never met so many whacked-out people in my whole life!"

The group roared with laughter.

I continued, trying to keep a straight face. "They may know all about mental health, but trust me, they don't know mental health. You wouldn't believe what's going on in their lives. It's a great place to hide."

The coach was cracking up. "Hilarious, John. As a coach, I have people screaming at me every game who think they know basketball but have probably never stepped foot on a basketball court."

The Culture

The principal was intrigued. "Knowing about something versus knowing something. I like that. Thinking this through, I see that developing leadership skills is somewhat analogous to being an athlete or a musician. Nobody ever learned how to swim or play the piano by reading a book. Nobody ever became a great golfer merely by watching Jack Nicklaus instructional videos. The knowledge must be applied and practiced."

"Precisely," the teacher explained. "The good news is that leadership is a skill, a learned ability. The bad news is that you do not develop leadership skills or character by going to reunions like this, attending seminars, reading books, or watching PowerPoint slides. It must be applied and practiced over time. The knowledge must go from your head to your heart and from your heart into your habits. It's a long journey from head to habit."

The nurse educated us a bit. "In one of my leadership classes at the hospital, we learned the neuroscience behind this idea. It was first explained some time ago by Daniel Goleman, the author who wrote extensively about emotional intelligence and character and why they are essential to leadership.

"We now know that character and emotional intelligence skills develop in the part of the brain known as the limbic system, which governs feelings, impulses, and drives.

"Contrast that to the neocortex, which governs analytical and technical ability, the part of the brain that grasps concepts and logic.

"We can learn how to read a balance sheet or how to do asset management by reading books or going to class. But we will never develop leadership or character skills doing those things.

"The limbic system learns best through desire, motivation, extended practice, feedback, and concerted effort. This explains why developing leadership skills is analogous

Chapter Six: Skill

to developing athletic or musical skills. The skills must be applied and practiced, yet very few leadership development programs grasp this crucial point."

The preacher wasn't buying any of it. "So, you folks really believe that anyone can be a great leader, huh? I didn't agree with that two years ago and don't agree with it now."

The guy was killing me.

The teacher patiently responded. "Lee, I think the point is the skill of leadership can be developed like any other skill. Some will develop and sharpen the skill better than others.

"I will never golf on the PGA Tour or play music with the New York Philharmonic. But I can learn to play golf or a musical instrument much better than I do today. Not everyone will develop the leadership skills to be a CEO or President of the United States. But we can significantly improve our leadership skills from where they are today.

"With knowledge, practice, and persistence, we can grow into better leaders, improve our character, and enhance the mark we leave upon others."

The teacher always gave me hope.

I was beginning to feel better.

Chapter Seven

POWER

*The value of coercive power
is inverse to its use.*

Robert Greenleaf

As I mentioned earlier, hope must be a good thing because it inspired me to share next.

"Simeon, two years ago you made the point that true leadership emanates from one's personal moral authority and not from management skills or positional power. On some level I know you are correct, though I must confess, as one skilled at manipulation and playing power games, I feel like a hypocrite even offering this one up."

The teacher smiled as he wrote:

Leadership ≠ Power

"Thank you, John. Your point is crucial because I do not believe anyone can truly grasp servant leadership unless you understand the distinction between having power over people versus having authority with people."

Predictably, the principal sought clarification. "I vaguely recall this power versus authority thing from last time, Simeon. Would you please refresh our memories?"

"Happy to, Theresa. Over a century ago, one of the founders of the field of sociology, Max Weber, differentiated between power and authority, and these definitions are still used widely today.

"Loosely defined, power is the ability to force or coerce others to do your will, even if they would choose not to, because of your position or might."

I added, "Allow me to paraphrase power for everyone. Power is 'do it or else.' Do it, or I'll write you up, fire you, spank you, or beat you up. Power is, I can make you do my will, whether you want to or not. Believe me; I know all about power."

The coach objected. "That definition makes power sound like a bad thing. Sometimes the leader has to take charge, tell people what to do, and define reality for them. I don't think power is necessarily bad."

"Nor do I," the teacher agreed, surprising a few of us. "There may be times when the leader must resort to power if that is what is needed because leaders always meet legitimate needs.

"But when power must be exercised, that should be a bad day for the leader. Why? Because the leader's personal authority or influence has broken down, requiring them to utilize their power. We will talk more about authority later."

"Hey, Greg," the preacher called out, "I'll bet you use some good old-fashioned power managing your troops, huh?"

The sergeant was composed. "Unfortunately, that is still true, sir. There are times when I must resort to positional power, but that is happening less and less these days now that I am learning to build authority with my soldiers.

"But as a point of clarification, sir, I do not manage my soldiers; I lead my soldiers. Can you imagine our fine soldiers being managed into battle? You manage things, sir. You lead people."

The preacher was clueless. "Sounds like semantics to me, my friend."

"It's anything but semantics, sir. It is the difference between leading people from the neck up or managing them from the neck down."

The preacher rolled his eyes. "Neck up, neck down, leaders, managers. Still not getting it, my friend."

The sergeant stayed on point. "Let me clarify, sir. Managing people from the neck down is simply renting people's hands, legs, and backs, and the labor market determines the price you have to pay for it. Managers bark orders and receive compliance for the rent they pay.

"Conversely, true leaders get people from the neck up. Those with the skill of leadership influence people to commit to and own the mission. True leaders inspire people and capture their hearts, minds, spirits, creativity, and excellence.

"Managers get compliance and mediocrity from their people. Leaders inspire commitment and excellence."

The teacher smiled. "Well put, Greg. In my decades of working in corporate America, I met many solid, effective managers who were utter failures as leaders. And I met some great leaders who were not particularly good managers."

The nurse quietly offered, "I'm sad to say that Detroit, my beloved hometown, is in an awful mess. My city was once a beautiful, vibrant, international port city with the highest per-capita income in the country. Now we are devastated and bankrupt, and I'm thinking most of our woes are due to a lot of power people who did not understand what Greg is saying. The good news is that things are slowly changing as new leadership has arrived."

The principal added, "Detroit's woes don't surprise me considering its hero, Henry Ford also used to say, 'Why is it every time I ask for a pair of hands, they come with a brain attached?' They even called employees 'hired hands' to dramatize the point. The message was clear: 'I don't want you to think, I want you to work. When I want your opinion, I will give it to you."

The sergeant chuckled. "Henry Ford used to say that you can have any color car you want as long as it's black. That was easy to say when there was little competition. After World War II, much of the civilized world was bombed to ruins, leveled, and ravaged by war. The United States' manufacturing machine had little competition."

Predictably, the principal shared a quote. "The Chinese have an old proverb that warns, 'When the gods wish to destroy us, they first give us thirty years of prosperity.'"

The nurse nodded. "I guess we had our thirty years of prosperity in Detroit, but then the world changed."

"Exactly, Kim," the sergeant agreed. "After the war, we sent these foreign countries some of our best and brightest people, and they actually listened to them. They learned, and developed new concepts, like continuous improvement, just-in-time, kanban, kaizen, Six Sigma, and lean manufacturing, to name a few."

The coach added, "And you can't do those things from the neck down. You've got to have people in the game and fully engaged. Perhaps one of the key lessons that Detroit missed along the way is that neck down isn't good enough. Not just hands and backs, but playing with their hearts, minds, spirits, creativity—all in."

Chapter Seven: Power

The sergeant pulled it together. "Here's the thing. We can hire any turkey to come in and play power games with people. Two-year-olds love to exercise power as they relentlessly order their family members and pets around the house. History is littered with clueless rulers, officers, and bosses.

"True leadership, on the other hand—inspiring and influencing people to contribute their best and taking ownership of the mission—requires a great deal of skill.

"Management skills, like planning, budgeting, problem-solving, organizing, reading balance sheets, and being strategic or tactical, are important skills but have little to do with leadership and inspiring people to action. Management is what you do. Leadership is who you are."

"Well put, Greg," Theresa affirmed. "I have known many school administrators who were talented at balancing budgets or developing curriculums but couldn't lead two people to the drinking fountain if their lives depended on it."

The coach laughed. "You go, girlfriend! And let's be empirically clear about this. By any definition of leadership you've got, if people aren't following, you're not leading. Vince Lombardi was fond of saying that once you've got their heart, the rest will go wherever you want to go."

The sergeant added, "Years ago in the military, neck-down was good enough, especially with a draft system supplying an endless stream of warm bodies. Now that it's a volunteer military, where getting fully trained recruits to reenlist is crucial. The neck down, 'do it or else' style isn't good enough anymore. Leaders must now be skilled in inspiring and influencing people to action and excellence. I have met many officers who were fit to manage but totally unfit to lead."

A light popped on for the nurse. "Of course! Over time, power damages relationships and healthy relationships are essential to maintaining a healthy organization."

"Great insight, Kim," the teacher quickly affirmed. "When power is used to dominate, control, and manipulate people, relationships are damaged, and ugly symptoms begin to emerge."

"Like?" the preacher pushed skeptically.

I leaped in with attitude. "I'm a power expert, Lee, so let me describe some of these symptoms to you. At work and at home, I'm living with the symptoms that come from low trust and broken relationships. How about rebellion, low commitment, morale issues, distrust, family dysfunction, organizational failure, labor strife, turnover, divorce, absenteeism, a PIP from my boss. Welcome to my life."

The preacher raised his arms. "Okay, got it. Relax, boss!"

The nurse's insight continued. "You may be able to squeak a few seasons out of power, but over time, abusive power erodes relationships. And life, including business, is all about relationships and people."

The principal added, "Of course it's all about people because without people there is no business. As Herb Kelleher, the founder and great servant leader at Southwest Airlines liked to say, 'The business of business is people.'

"What is becoming clear to me is, as leaders, we need to be very careful about breaking things like trust and relationships. We're going to be doing family and work for more than a few seasons."

The nurse was totally getting it. "And once you break trust and the relationship, the results are mere compliance. Their attitude is now, 'You've got me from the neck down until I can get away from you, you toxic person you.'"

The teacher summed up. "As we discussed this morning, people today have a low tolerance for power people. In fact, the whole world has grown weary and is rebelling against power people.

Chapter Seven: Power

"In short, my friends, if you are building your leadership style on power, it is a house of cards. Over time, trust will be damaged, relationships will deteriorate, and the foundation for a healthy, functioning team will be compromised or lost.

"Power alone is simply not sustainable."

It was lunchtime, and everyone but the preacher hustled over to the dining lodge. The preacher said he wanted to spend time alone in his room, which suited me fine.

Like the training room, the dining area had giant windows along the west wall, capturing the stunning view of Lake Michigan. The smaller windows on the east wall revealed a beautiful cobblestone pathway leading into a dense and dark pine forest.

I made a mental note to check out that path before departing on Sunday evening.

The dining area was spacious and simply furnished with large round tables. Simeon explained that only round tables were used by the monks during any group gatherings, including meals and monastic meetings, to symbolize their equality.

Apparently, this tradition was borrowed from the legend of King Arthur and the Round Table, dating back over a thousand years. It seems that King Arthur insisted upon the round table to dramatize and reinforce the equal status of the group members. The First Among Equals concept arose from this tradition.

The teacher further explained that King Arthur was still the king, with all the burdens and obligations inherent in that role while the knights had their own unique duties and responsibilities. Yet all were expected to assume

The Culture

leadership responsibility for the success and safety of the group, regardless of position. All were equally responsible.

"A leaderless group?" I questioned skeptically.

"Not leaderless, John. A group of all leaders."

Chapter Eight

AUTHORITY

The spirit of servant leadership is the spirit of moral authority.

Stephen R. Covey

The teacher grabbed a chef's hat and apron before getting to work slicing and dicing veggies along with mixing some tasty dips for us to munch on.

I asked, "Can I do something, Simeon? Despite all my issues, I'm actually pretty good in the kitchen."

The teacher tossed me an apron. "I would love your help, John."

In under thirty minutes, the two of us managed to create a scrumptious buffet, complete with lunchmeat, soup, fresh bread, two salads, iced tea, and lemonade. To top it off, the teacher reached into the refrigerator and pulled out two large pies, cherry and pecan, that he had baked early that morning.

As the group marveled at our creation, the coach

The Culture

proclaimed, "Behold, the feast. Compliments to the monk and the manager."

The manager label stung. I turned to Chris and feebly replied, "Someday soon, I hope it will be the monk and the leader."

The coach looked like someone had just shot her dog.

"I'm so sorry, John. I didn't mean anything by calling you the manager. I still don't have my lingo straight."

"No worries, I'm good," I quickly responded, hiding the sting. "Let's dig in!"

Following lunch, the principal was raring to go. "Before lunch, Simeon said, 'We will never fully grasp servant leadership until we understand that leadership is not built upon positional power, but rather upon personal authority.' I would like to continue that dialogue."

The teacher wrote:

Leadership = Authority (Influence)

"Thank you, Theresa, for keeping this thread going. To review, our German sociologist-friend, Max Weber, defined power as the ability to force or coerce others to do your will.

"Weber then defines authority as the skill of getting people to willingly act because of your personal influence. The paraphrase for power is 'do it or else' while the paraphrase for authority is 'I'll do it willingly for you.'"

The principal added, "I just looked up authority on my phone and discovered that the root word, author, is defined as one who creates, originates, or gives existence to something."

Chapter Eight: Authority

The teacher smiled. "That is a perfect lead in, Theresa. Your authority, your personal influence, is something you have created, something you have authored, something that resides within you."

"Of course!" the coach excitedly joined in. "This makes perfect sense. Our positional power does not reside or originate from within us personally. If you are my boss in the working world, you would have no power over me if the organization did not give it to you. A police officer, military officer, or bench judge only exercises the power entrusted to them by the people. As a coach, I am merely a steward of the positional power on loan to me from the university."

The principal added, "Come to think of it, we still use these definitions of power and authority today. Think of politicians who get caught in various scams and sexual escapades, and the media talking heads say things like, 'The senator has lost their moral authority to influence and serve their constituents.' Another example would be the Catholic church, with critics claiming the church is losing its moral authority with the priest scandals."

Her comments resonated with me. "You can have power over people and yet have little or no influence, authority, with people. I'm a living example. Just ask my boss, who may soon be my ex-boss, or my wife if she's still there, or my kids if you can get them to talk to you."

Did I say that?

The teacher looked directly at me. "That was a very vulnerable thing to say, John."

The preacher interjected, "My thinking on authority is—"

The teacher shocked us by interrupting him mid-sentence.

"Excuse me, but I feel moved to speak. I must say that I am disappointed by the group dynamics I am witnessing.

The Culture

A few times today, John has taken risks and shared some difficult things that the group has chosen to ignore. This strikes me as odd for people who claim to care about one another."

The crickets began chirping.

"It's okay, Simeon," I announced, feeling awkward and wanting to rescue everyone from their misery.

More crickets.

The nurse looked my way. "You are right, Simeon. I'm sorry, John."

"I'm good," I mumbled. "Let's just move on."

The sergeant obliged. "History provides many examples of people who had no power yet wielded great authority. I'm thinking of people like Gandhi, Martin Luther King Jr., Nelson Mandela, Mother Teresa, and Jesus. No positional power but a ton of world-changing authority."

The coach interjected, "Greg, I think historical cases of authority are helpful, but I prefer real-life stories that I can better relate to. Can anyone cite personal examples of this principle of authority and influence?"

"I can," Theresa quickly responded. "In my first teaching job out of college, the principal was one tough cookie who demanded excellence. She never allowed us teachers to be mediocre and pushed us to give our best. She was all about the kids and focused on the mission. She would regularly take time to sit in our classes and provide respectful yet insightful feedback that was sometimes difficult to hear.

"But most importantly, she cared. She was truly interested in me, and I trusted her. I could talk to her about anything, and I would have walked over hot coals for her. Even today, although she obviously has no power over me, she still has authority with me. I would be there in a heartbeat if she ever needed me."

Chapter Eight: Authority

The sergeant was nodding. "For me, an example of authority would be my mother. She was one tough lady. Thankfully, she no longer has power over me because I can finally run faster than she can!"

We all laughed, but tears began to roll down the sergeant's cheeks. "But here's the thing. I would do anything for my mother. She served me, and she served her family. My father passed when I was six, and Mom worked two and sometimes three jobs to support my four brothers and me. She hugged hard and spanked hard as she served and sacrificed for us through thick and thin. And believe me, I was a pretty tough kid to serve."

The nurse coughed. "No offense, Greg, but we experienced some of your rough edges two years ago."

"None taken, ma'am. Yet, no matter what, my mother always had my back. She served me. So, although my mother has no power over me, she still possesses great authority with me."

The coach was touched. "I love that, Greg. I had a high school volleyball coach named Phyllis who took me under her wing when I was a confused and angry teenager. She taught me about character, discipline, team, life, boys, and so many other things. To this day, I wonder where I would be if I had not run into Phyllis. I would do anything for Coach Phyllis, then and now."

The teacher looked pleased. "Wonderful examples. Authority, then, is your personal influence with others, that indelible mark you leave on people. And this influence is built, earned, through service and sacrifice.

"Here's another way to look at power and authority. Power can be bought and sold, given and taken away. Conversely, authority is never bought or sold, never given or taken away. Authority is about who you are as a person. Can I trust you? Are you committed? Do you care about me?

"Do your people willingly submit to your leadership? If so, you have built true authority, the essence of leadership."

"And if not," the sergeant added, "you only have them from the neck down, their compliance, until they can get away from you."

"That's correct, Greg. So, in the macro, everyone is a leader because everyone influences and impacts other people every day. Customers, employees, suppliers, vendors, one another. We all leave a mark."

The nurse's face lit up. "I love this idea! Our leadership is the mark we leave on the people and organizations we come into contact with. We all leave a mark, either good or bad.

"So, the question is not, 'Are you a leader?' The real question is, 'Are you effective?'

"Do you have influence, authority, with others? Do you make the organization better? Do you leave things better than you found them? Will people be glad you were there?'"

The teacher nodded and smiled.

"This is the true essence of leadership, Kim."

Chapter Nine

SERVING

*Everyone can be great
because anybody can serve.
You don't need a college degree to serve—
You only need a heart full of grace.
A soul generated by love.*

Martin Luther King Jr.

The teacher scanned the room for the next contributor to our growing list.

"I guess I'll go," the preacher halfheartedly volunteered. "As a pastor, I guess I would be negligent if I didn't say that leadership is about serving others. After all, the leader of my chosen faith, Jesus Christ, said that to lead is to serve. If the premise is that leadership is influence, by definition, Jesus was a great leader because He influenced a lot of people over the past two thousand years."

The teacher turned and wrote:

Leadership = Serving

The Culture

The teacher threw out a bone. "So how does serving others impact our authority and influence?"

The sergeant bit. "It's simply the Law of the Harvest; we reap what we sow. When we serve others by identifying and meeting their legitimate needs, most people will naturally feel grateful, even indebted, and will want to give back.

"I don't know why it took me so long to grasp this simple truth. If you get your people what they need, they will get you everything you need.

"Serving your people is simply giving them what they need to raise their game and be successful. And when you serve people, it gets their attention, their loyalty, and they naturally want to reciprocate."

The nurse shared next. "I once had a mentor who regularly reminded us nurse managers that our leadership would never be defined by what we accomplished. Rather, our leadership would be defined by what we got accomplished through other people. She told us to take care of our people, serve them, and get them what they needed, and they would amaze us with what they were capable of accomplishing."

The principal nodded. "A wise woman. Serving and sacrificing by extending ourselves for others is the universal language everyone understands. Perhaps that is why great servant leaders have such a profound impact on our world. Through their service and sacrifice, they inspire others to action and to excellence."

Becoming predictable, the preacher wasn't so sure. "That's all fine and dandy but you have to be careful about doing what people want. Believe me, people will walk all over you if you let them. I've seen some ugly things take place in business, and even in the church, since I've become a part of that world."

The sergeant countered. "Sir, serving people means

Chapter Nine: Serving

meeting their needs, not their wants. Slaves do what people want. Servants do what people need. What my employees or my children want may be much different than what they need."

The preacher reacted skeptically. "Here we go with the semantics again, my friend. Needs and wants? I'm not seeing the difference."

"Sir, in my view there is a vast distinction between needs and wants. For me, a want is a wish or a desire without regard to the consequences.

"My direct report may want to take a two-hour lunch break or my son may want to stay out until three in the morning. But as the leader, I must be concerned with the consequences of the behavior. Allowing a two-hour break will create disharmony in the team, and bad things can happen to kids at three o'clock in the morning."

"Great point, Greg!" the principal exclaimed. "And as we said earlier, our leadership is defined by whether people leave us better off than when they arrived. Letting people get away with bad behavior is not serving them in the long run. It may be what they want, but is not what they need."

The preacher pushed further. "So what's a need?"

The sergeant thought for a minute. "For me, a need is a legitimate physical or psychological requirement for the well-being of the people I lead. When I make people decisions, I try to run it through this filter: 'Is this a legitimate need or a want? Is this request in the long-term best interests of the individual or the organization?'"

The preacher objected. "Seriously, sarge? Let's be real here. Doesn't this 'meeting needs' and 'serving' jazz go against the military style of command and control?"

"To the contrary, sir. You may be surprised to hear that the English word 'sergeant' originates from the Latin word 'serviens,' meaning one who serves. My rank of sergeant reminds me daily that my job description is all about serving."

The preacher mumbled something incoherent.

The principal suddenly lit up. "Here's another quote for you all. My namesake, Mother Teresa of Calcutta, used to say that love has to be put into action, and that action is service."

The teacher liked it. "Yes, Theresa. Our service to others is simply love in action. The last time we were together, we developed a working definition of love. Does anyone remember what we came up with?"

The nurse was all over it. "How could we forget? I know it by heart. We defined love as a verb, the act of extending yourself for others by identifying and meeting their legitimate needs and seeking their greatest good."

She continued. "I had always thought of love as an emotion rather than something I actively choose to do for another person. But since we last met, I have come to understand romance and passion as the language of love, the expression of love, and even the fruit of love.

"But emotional feelings are not the substance of love because love is what we actually do for others, not how we feel. Again, love is a verb first. Love is our willingness to extend ourselves for others. To paraphrase, love is as love does."

The sergeant agreed. "I'll say, Kim. I've known guys who talk about how much they love their wives one day but chase other women the next. Or they tell me how much they love their kids but can't carve out an hour a week of quality time with them. People may say the right things, but is love as love says? Is love as love feels? No. I believe you are correct, young lady. Love is as love does."

"Excellent!" the teacher exclaimed. "It's effortless to say we love our spouse, friends, or family members. It's easy to

Chapter Nine: Serving

say that our employees are our greatest asset. In fact, every CEO I've ever known has said that very thing. People say the right things, but in the end, what separates people is not what they say but what they do. Our actions always betray what we truly believe.

"I worry our culture is butchering the classical definition of love by emotionalizing and sexualizing it, as opposed to conveying the message that authentic love extends and gives of itself."

I snickered. "Hollywood emotional love is easy love. Heck, when I was eighteen, I could fall in love five different times on a Friday night. And the more beer I drank, the more in love I got!"

Everyone laughed except the preacher, who chose to preach instead.

"When the Bible challenges us to 'Love our neighbor,' the verb in the sentence is love. There is a timeless definition of love I read at every wedding I conduct, the same definition that has been read at millions of weddings around the world for the past two-thousand years. This love definition was written twenty centuries ago by a Jewish man named Paul and is one of the most famous passages in all of literature."

"Hang on; I've got it," the nurse said, digging through her purse. "I have the definition of love imprinted on my hospital ID lanyard… if I can just find… here it is. Love is patient, kind, humble, respectful, selfless, forgiving, honest, and fully committed."

"And there are absolutely no feelings on that list," the sergeant observed. "That famous two-thousand-year-old list not only defines love but beautifully details the qualities of personal character and leadership."

The coach jumped in. "Vince Lombardi, the late, great football coach, regularly told his players that though they

The Culture

might not like each other at times, as their coach he would love them, adding, 'And my love for you will be relentless!'

"I think Lombardi demonstrated his love for them by pushing them to be the best they could possibly be. When they left his team, they would be in demand in the NFL. Remember the test of leadership. Are people better when they leave than when they arrived?"

I surprised myself by adding, "And sometimes you have to love people you don't like. There are times when I'm pretty sure my wife doesn't like me very much. Check that, times when I know she can't stand me. Yet she still demonstrates her love through patience, kindness, forgiveness, and solid commitment. She's still in the game even though I may be acting like a jerk, which seems to be most of the time these days."

"In the end," the nurse added, "Love is extending yourselves for others, serving them, and treating them the way you would want to be treated. Living the golden rule. I don't think I have ever met anyone who disagreed with that rule."

"That's right, Kim," the sergeant agreed. "Be the boss you wish your boss would be. The person you want your boss to be is the same person your people want you to be. Be the mother or father you wish your mother or father had been more fully for you. Be the neighbor you wish your neighbor would be."

The teacher summed up. "So, the formula for leading is simple. Serve others by identifying and meeting their legitimate needs. This service will build relationships and your personal authority. Our success in life, whether personal or professional, is ultimately relational."

I couldn't resist. "I'm learning this truth the hard way. At work, healthy relationships equal healthy business. Bad relationships equal bad business. At home, healthy relationships equal healthy family. Dysfunctional relationships equals dysfunctional family. Do you think I will ever get it?"

"I do, John." the teacher encouragingly replied. "And how do you have healthy relationships with people? By identifying and meeting their legitimate needs, which requires service and sacrifice."

"To lead is to serve. It remains one of life's greatest paradoxical truths."

Chapter Ten

COACHING

*They call it coaching, but it is teaching.
You don't just tell them it is so,
but you show them the reasons why it is so.
And you repeat and repeat and repeat,
until they are convinced—until they know.*

Coach Vince Lombardi

Of the six students, only the coach had yet to contribute. The sergeant looked her way. "Lay some wisdom on us, young lady."

"Well, you will be shocked to hear me say I believe coaching is essential to effective leadership."

"Defend your position, coach," the teacher challenged as he wrote:

> Leadership = Coaching

She was ready.

"For me, a great coach or leader is one who motivates,

The Culture

guides, and inspires their people to dig down and give their very best for the team and the mission."

"And this coaching process essentially involves executing the three F's, something I learned years ago at a coaching clinic."

The principal and nurse reacted in unison. "The three F's?"

"Here's how it works. The first F is for foundation, which means setting the standard and clearly defining expectations. The leader must be crystal clear when setting the bar because everything that follows is executed against that standard or foundation."

"So, the first F is setting the ground rules?" the nurse questioned. "As Theresa said earlier, every team member has two subconscious questions, 'How am I supposed to behave, and what happens if I don't?'"

"Exactly, Kim. The second F is for feedback. As people perform against the set standards, the leader must now provide feedback around observed gaps between the standard and the actual performance. And this feedback must be timely and candid."

The nurse thought it through aloud. "So, if I'm performing above the standard, the leader provides feedback in the form of appreciation, recognition, and rewards, correct? And if I'm performing below the standard, the leader provides feedback and coaching to get me to the required standard or above?"

Chris nodded. "That's the essence of it, Kim.

"Which brings us to the third F, which is creating friction or the necessary tension to expand and grow the positive gaps and eliminate the negative gaps. Which is why the leader must be so direct and clear in setting the standards and expectations, especially when confronting negative gaps. You can't be writing speeding tickets if the

Chapter Ten: Coaching

speed limit signs are not clearly posted."

"How do you create this friction for the negative gaps?" the nurse asked softly, sounding intimidated.

The sergeant was all over it. "In the military, we utilize the three E's when corrective action or friction is needed."

"Definition, please," the principal demanded.

"Yes, ma'am. The first E is establishing the gap. This crucial first step requires defining the gap between the set standard and the observed performance. This requires the leader, to be fully prepared to clearly and unemotionally articulate the observed deficiencies. It is crucial that the leader does their homework—or discovery, as an attorney might say—prior to the intervention."

The principal was nodding. "Establish the gap. Pretty basic but pretty important. I mean, how can we fix something unless we first get agreement that an issue exists?"

"Precisely, ma'am. The second E is exploring the reasons for the gap. The step requires active listening on the part of the leader to ensure it is a discipline problem, rather than something else. This is where the interviewee gets their day in court.

"The leader must exercise restraint to silence themselves during this phase of the interview process, which includes resisting the urge to speak when the interviewee is silent. I have learned valuable information following periods of awkward silence when I have made room for them to speak first. Remember, they need to do the explaining. It's their gap, not your gap."

"Great stuff, Greg," I encouraged, scribbling notes as quickly as I could.

"The third E is eliminating the gap. This requires an action plan detailing the specific behaviors and actions that must change, dates and times for follow-up meetings, and the clearly stated consequences if the gap fails to close.

Proper execution of all three E's is essential."

The principal was delighted. "I love this, Greg, because none of what you have outlined needs to be emotional. There doesn't need to be weeping and gnashing of teeth, because it is fact-based, all business, rather than personal."

"Yes, that's the beauty of it, Kim. The discipline process is simply, 'Here is our standard and here is your performance. We've got a gap. As your leader, I am here to understand the reasons for the gap and help you to raise your game. If the gap does not go away, I will have to escalate.'"

The nurse confessed. "I struggle with confronting people and holding them accountable. I don't like conflict or having tension with people."

What followed blew me away.

The sergeant looked intently at the nurse and said, "I care about you, Kim, which is why I am going to take a risk here. May I be candid with you?"

"Of course, Greg," she quickly replied.

"So here's the thing. If I work for you, and you won't tell me the truth about my performance, we do not have an honest or an authentic relationship. In fact, our relationship is deceitful because you are pretending everything is okay when it's not okay. Do you agree so far, Kim?"

"Ouch, but I do, Greg," the nurse softly replied.

"Now, please don't tell me how much you care about me if you're not willing to have me mad at you for a couple of days. If you really cared about me, you would be kicking my rear end up and over that performance bar every day, so that when I leave you, I will be better than when I arrived. Do you agree, Kim."

"I do," she faintly responded.

"Please hear this, Kim. I don't need another buddy. I need a leader, and that's what you signed up to do. Your truth about my performance may not be what I want to

Chapter Ten: Coaching

hear, but it is exactly what I need to hear."

The crickets were chirping again.

After a minute or so, the nurse firmly replied, "It's hard for me to hear this, but you are absolutely right, Greg. Thank you for having the courage to say that to me.

"And as I am thinking this through, I think it's interesting that, as a mother, I have no problem confronting and holding my children accountable. So, it seems odd I would have a hard time doing it at work."

"Kim, I'm curious," the teacher inquired. "What motivates you to hold your children accountable?"

Moments of thoughtful silence had passed before the nurse had the answer. "I guess because I love them so much. I want what's best for them."

"What a beautiful and honest answer, Kim," the teacher responded. "This same principle, this same motivation, is what drives great leadership. We tell our people the truth because we care about them and want what is best for them. We don't do them any favors when we fail to tell them the truth. We love them by telling them the truth."

The sergeant had more. "The command chief at our base regularly reminds our leadership team that if we don't hold people accountable for excellence, we are, in effect, thieves and liars."

"I think that's a bit strong," the preacher protested.

"I don't think it is, sir. Look at the facts. If you are in a leadership position in an organization, and you do not hold people accountable for excellence, you are stealing every time you take a paycheck. You are being paid to hold people accountable. Furthermore, when you fail to tell your people the truth, you are lying, pretending everything is okay when it clearly is not okay."

The principal agreed. "And there is a lot at stake because there are winners and losers, in the military, business, or

The Culture

in any organization for that matter. Even in my school district, I think of how many of our children are suffering because many school administrators simply will not tell teachers the truth about their performance."

Even the nurse jumped in. "Anyone who doesn't believe that there are winners and losers should come visit me in Detroit, and I'll show you how devastating bad leadership is to people and their communities.

"I mean think about it. How many spouses, sons, daughters, suppliers, vendors, customers, or other businesses are counting on your organization to provide for their futures? And you are willing to put all of that at risk because you don't want to tell someone the truth about their performance?"

I do believe the nurse was starting to get it.

Feeling inspired, I also jumped in. "Other than the competition, who benefits when we don't hold people accountable for excellence? Does the person we are dealing with benefit? Obviously not because they will be worse off when they leave than when they arrived."

The nurse came full circle. "I suppose the only one who 'benefits' when I don't hold people accountable is me. I can avoid the hassle and any uncomfortable tension with my people by simply withholding the truth. That is not a servant leader. That is a self-serving leader. Yuck!"

The sergeant was touched. "You're awesome, Kim. And remember, discipline is not about chastising or punishing people, which is how I used to look at discipline.

"To the contrary. When I discipline, I am helping my people, teaching them and coaching them, to be the best they can be. When I see a gap between how they are performing and how they should be performing, I look at it as an opportunity to help them raise their game. It's another opportunity to serve them."

The principal added, "I just looked up discipline on my phone and the definition is all about teaching and training. It says discipline comes from the Latin word *discipulus*, the same word from which disciple is derived.

"Perhaps that's a better way of thinking about it. Discipline is not about punishing people; it's about discipling them to excellence, teaching and coaching them to become their very best."

The nurse wanted more. "One last question on friction. How do you know when it's time to pull the plug on someone and remove them from the team?"

The teacher was all over that one. "I would always ask myself three questions before pulling the plug.

"Question one: Is there anything else I can do to help them succeed?

"Question two: Is there another seat on the bus where they can be successful, and does it make sense to make that change?

"Question three: If the person resigned today, would I try to talk them out of it or rehire them?

"When my answer to those three questions was no, it was time to do my job as the leader."

"Time to share them with the competition!" the sergeant bellowed.

Chapter Eleven

MORE COACHING
(HUGGING & SPANKING)

I love you, Jeff…
I'm your biggest fan!

You just had the worst year in the company…
I'm going to take you out if you can't get it fixed!

Jack Welch to Jeffrey Immelt
Former General Electric CEO to
GE subordinate (current GE CEO)

Now it was the sergeant's turn to confess.
"Kim, you honestly shared your struggle with creating friction and holding people accountable. I have a confession to make as well.

"Prior to our retreat two years ago, I viewed leadership as simply driving people to accomplish tasks by whatever means necessary, including and especially through coercion and power. The old me was all about accomplishing tasks, just getting it done, with no thought given to the relationship or the feelings of others.

The Culture

"I have learned, painfully, that this approach is simply not sustainable. If I accomplish tasks at the expense of the relationship, I will ultimately fail. As we have discussed, damaged relationships and broken trust result in neck-down compliance. I have learned, the hard way, that excellence comes from commitment, not compliance.

"I now know that leadership is about inspiring and influencing people to action, to excellence, and making it sustainable over time. So, my focus is still on accomplishing tasks, but I'm also focused on meeting needs and building relationships for the future."

The principal agreed. "I've known many a manager who could accomplish tasks, 'just get 'er done,' as you put it, Greg, but the emotional bloodshed and collateral damage was not sustainable."

"On the other hand," I hopped in, "the working world is littered with managers who think leadership is about making everyone happy. They believe that they are effective leaders when there are no issues or tension with anybody. They seem to believe that as long as everyone is happy, that is all that matters, even if we go out of business."

That resonated with the coach. "This is making perfect sense to me. Accomplishing tasks while we build relationships for the future. As was said earlier, it doesn't take any skill or courage to yell and boss people around. We can hire any clueless dictator or emotional two-year-old to come in and exercise power."

I said, "On the flip side, we can hire any music major to come in and sing 'Kumbaya' to everyone. What I'm learning is that the real skill lies with the person who can come in and accomplish both: accomplish tasks while building healthy relationships for the future. Who can find the sweet spot between the hugging and the spanking. Now that's a skill and one I hope to one day possess."

Chapter Eleven: More Coaching (Hugging & Spanking)

The preacher couldn't resist. "Spanking? That's a bit crude."

I stayed calm. "Relax, Lee. Spanking is just a metaphor for being dedicated to the truth and providing the necessary consequences as needed."

"I like it, John," the sergeant interjected. "I lead by serving my people. And I serve them by hugging them when they need a hug and spanking them when they need a spank, meeting their needs so they can become their very best."

On cue, the principal wanted clarity. "Greg, I get the spanking part with your three E's and Chris' three F's. Exactly what do you mean by the hugging?"

"I guess I would define hugging as actions that communicate to my people I truly respect and care about them. Actions that show I value them personally."

The principal wanted more. "Real life examples, please?"

Greg thought for a minute. "I hug my people by building a relationship with them, by treating them like important people, and by taking the time to sincerely appreciate them and their contributions to the mission."

The principal added, "Mother Teresa used to say that people crave appreciation more than they crave bread. And that woman saw lots of very hungry people. Appreciation is a deep human need."

"I now know that," the sergeant admitted. "I used to believe being nice and giving appreciation was namby-pamby nonsense, reserved for weak leaders."

"As did I," I confessed. "I thought it was enough to tell my wife I loved her when I married her, and if that ever changed, I would get back to her. Who can blame her for wanting to leave me."

The sergeant turned solemn. "There is an old saying in the military that a soldier wouldn't give you their life for

The Culture

a million dollars, but will fight to the death for a small, colored ribbon, a little appreciation from their country."

The principal added, "Gandhi said gratitude was the mother of all virtues. Respect is also up there as a huge human need. When we fail to give people respect, we make a huge withdrawal out of their emotional bank account. And disrespecting people is especially costly. People may forget what you said, but they will never forget how you made them feel."

"Tell me more, Greg. How else do you hug?"

"I make the time to meet with, talk with, and truly listen to my people. For example, I schedule private face time with each of my direct reports a minimum of once each month."

I was impressed. "Wow! Where do you find the time, Greg? And what the heck do you talk about?"

"Regarding time, it only takes twenty minutes per session, so with ten directs, I conduct one session every other day, a very small percentage of my time.

"Regarding content, I simply ask five open-ended questions which they know in advance. Question one, what is going well? Two, what is not going well? Three, what are you doing to improve as a leader? Four, what are you doing to improve the organization? And, five, what can I do to help?

"I then work to truly listen to their answers, which often sends us off on important tangents. People tell me I listen better than I used to, but I'm not so sure. I know I can do better. But I now realize I used to listen with the intent to reply rather than with the intent to understand."

"That is so me!" I burst out. "When someone's talking to me, I'm usually thinking, 'When are you going to stop talking so I can give you the right answer?' or 'How can I manipulate this conversation to the way I want it to go?'

Chapter Eleven: More Coaching (Hugging & Spanking)

I probably hear very little of what others are really trying to say to me."

The sergeant shook his head. "Been there, my friend. Now that doesn't mean I always agree with what others are saying or that I give in easily. What it does mean is that I work harder to understand their point of view. I try to see it as they see it and feel it as they feel it."

"I think the precise word for this is empathy," the principal interjected.

"People have a deep need to be heard," the nurse suggested. "Having empathy for people does not mean agreeing or fixing things for them. But it helps the relationship immensely when we do the work to listen and understand. What better way is there to give respect to someone?"

"That reminds me of a small plaque in my wife, the shrink's, office: *What most people need is a good listening to.*" I smirked, but craved more.

"Any other ways you hug, Greg? God only knows, I need lots of pointers."

"Oh, there are lots of little things. I work to give more encouragement to people than I used to. I also developed a system to acknowledge birthdays, anniversaries, length of service, and other important dates.

"One of the things I love to do is send letters to the parents of my soldiers, thanking them for raising such a great person. It amazes me the impact that small effort has on people."

The nurse was enthralled. "Greg, I'm amazed with how much you have changed over the past two years. Congratulations."

"Thank you, Kim. I have a long way to go. In the end, I think the essence of hugging is paying attention and caring for your people. As corny as it sounds, it's the little things like kindness that make a house a home."

The Culture

"Kindness is the WD-40 of human relationships," the principal quoted. "And it doesn't cost a thing."

The preacher inappropriately butted in again. "Okay, enough of the soft skills stuff. Let's move on."

The sergeant gazed steadily at the preacher. "Sir, now that you say it, what an irony that business folks refer to relational skills as the soft skills. I no longer believe that. Learning and applying these new skills has been some of the hardest work I have ever done."

"I agree, Greg," the coach seconded. "What do you think would be more difficult: teaching someone how to read a balance sheet or learning how to empathize with another human being? Teaching someone to manage inventory or developing relationships and building trust with a group of people?"

"No question about it. This is the hard stuff."

"It is, Chris," the sergeant continued. "As I mentioned two years ago, I was all about kicking butts and taking names, with little tolerance for holding hands and singing songs. Today, I am much more relationally oriented, yet, ironically, I am firmer and more direct with my people than I have ever been."

"I'm confused," the principal interjected. "Softer but tougher?"

"In a word, Theresa, I have become assertive. This part is huge. Before, I was aggressive, which means that I was open, honest, and direct, but my overbearing behavior and words violated other people's rights. Now, I am open, honest, and direct but respectful, and I work hard to never violate the rights of others. I never personalize it but work to keep it respectful and professional. It has done wonders for my leadership."

It was a perfect lead-in for Simeon. "Greg is touching upon another paradoxical truth about leadership. The great leaders that I have known possess the dual character

Chapter Eleven: More Coaching (Hugging & Spanking)

qualities of softness and toughness. They are passionate in their love for people and extend themselves to build solid relationships. Yet, they are equally passionate when it comes to pursuing individual and organizational excellence."

The teacher continued. "The great servant leaders I know, are anything but wimps. In fact, I would describe them as pit bulls. Using our metaphor, they are relentless at both the hugging and the spanking.

"On the hugging side, they know it's all about people. Consequently, when it's time to show respect, give appreciation, listen, build relationships, or celebrate success, the great servant leaders were all in. When it's time for the company picnic or Christmas party, they are the first ones in line shouting, 'Let's party!'

"Conversely, when it's time to be tough, whether that's holding people accountable for standards, driving excellence, watching out for the bottom line, or insisting upon continuous improvement, the great servant leaders were all in.

"The essence of great leadership is finding that sweet spot between the hugging and the spanking. This amazing skill is certainly not something you are born with. It is developed with great care and practice, choice by choice. What an awesome privilege it is to work with and for a leader who is operating in that zone."

"Awesome while it lasts," Theresa sullenly added. "Great servant leaders can ruin you for life. Early in my career, I worked for someone just as you're describing, and my world was heavenly for four years. It was life changing and my fondest career memory.

"The downside came when she got promoted and moved on. Her replacement was a real piece of work. The contrast was devastating."

Chapter Twelve

CHARACTER

*Character is the person you are
in the dark when nobody is looking.*

Dwight Moody

It was mid-afternoon, and the teacher graciously cut us loose for a sixty-minute break, reminding us that the kitchen was well stocked.

The group moved quickly toward the door, behaving like addicts as they frantically fumbled for their various electronic devices.

Resisting that urge, I chose to explore the cobblestone pathway I had scoped out from the dining room earlier and quickly found myself in a dense pinewood forest.

The cobblestone portion soon ended and became a cushy trail. I felt like I was walking on foam rubber, probably from the accumulation of fallen pine needles over many centuries. The fragrance beneath the canopy of giant trees was intoxicating.

The Culture

The quietness of the place was deafening and foreign, causing me to reflect upon the vast amounts of noise and distractions that had become my life. Lost in my thoughts, I followed the beautiful winding trail deep into the forest.

After some time, I stopped and took one final look down the trail, which meandered into the darkness. I turned to head back, not wanting to be late for our afternoon session. Out of nowhere, strong emotions again began stirring, irritating me. I figured I had emoted enough for the next quarter century.

But hearing these truths about leadership and juxtaposing them with my life was overwhelming. My chest again tightened as I dropped to my knees, struggling to no avail to hold back yet another emotional outburst.

Back in class, the teacher requested we sit in silence for several minutes. Most of my classmates appeared comfortable with the silence, but I was not.

And judging by how he was squirming in his chair, I gathered the preacher wasn't too fond of silence either.

Just when I thought the preacher would spontaneously combust, he practically shouted, "So, moving right along…"

Before I could verbally smack him, the nurse came to the rescue yet again. "We haven't heard from you, Simeon. What is missing from our list?"

The teacher walked slowly toward the whiteboard appearing to be in deep thought. He wrote:

Leadership = Character

Simeon asked for input.

Chapter Twelve: Character

The sergeant blurted out, "Leadership is character put into action."

"Greg, please define your terms," the principal insisted.

"Happy to oblige, ma'am. Character is doing the right thing, even when you don't feel like doing it or doing it comes with a cost. In fact, I am not sure it can be an act of character unless it costs you something.

"Character is winning those wars, those internal battles between what you want to do and what you should do. Character is your moral maturity."

"Wow, well put, Greg," I reacted, scribbling notes.

The sergeant wasn't finished. "Character is the courage to do the right thing in the face of pressure or inclinations to behave otherwise. Character is the courage to do the right thing even though people might not like it or may get upset with you. The difficult part of life is not knowing the right thing to do. The difficult part of life is doing it."

The nurse softly objected. "But leadership is a skill, a learned or acquired ability. Isn't character and personality something we're basically born with?"

Here was a topic I knew something about.

"My better half, the shrink, has often told me that personality and character are two very different things. She could give any of us a quick Myers-Briggs test or DISC profile and tell us our personality type. You've all heard labels like introvert or extrovert, dominant or passive, thinking or feeling, et cetera. She says the experts generally agree that personality is established at an early age."

Nodding, the nurse said, "I would agree with that. You don't go to a seminar or read a book and move from a Type A to a Type B personality."

"Exactly," I continued. "Psychologists generally agree personality is pretty well fixed by age six and IQ by around age fifteen. But not so with character, hence the term

81

maturity, 'moral maturity' to use Greg's words. I take that to mean our will, our choices, combined with actions to do the right thing. And these choices and actions become our habits over time."

"Well said, my friend!" the sergeant exclaimed. "We could use you in the military."

"The way things are going, I may enlist," I laughed, only half-kidding.

The sergeant had more. "Leadership is all about character, not style or personality. Just look at great leaders in history, and you'll see very different personalities and styles. Take coaches like John Wooden versus Bobby Knight. Or business leaders like Steve Jobs and Mary Kay. Or military leaders like General Eisenhower and General Patton. Or spiritual leaders like Billy Graham and Martin Luther King Jr. They all had very different personalities and styles yet were effective leaders in their unique way."

The nurse wasn't sure. "So, you're saying that personality is set early in life, yet character is pliable and changing. But aren't we all born basically good? With good character? Isn't that our real nature?"

The preacher laughed out loud. "Born good? Did anyone ever have to teach their kids to be bad? Instruct them on how to be selfish? Train them in how to tell lies? I don't think so. These things were all quite natural. We *teach* our kids character."

"Great point, Lee," the teacher exclaimed, which, honestly, made me a little jealous. "My view would be that human beings have a remarkably consistent idea of good and bad, right and wrong, a moral sense, if you will.

"But that is very different from saying we are born good. Our innate moral sense competes with other innate urges like self-centeredness and getting our own way. Life relentlessly bombards us with stimulus, and we must

Chapter Twelve: Character

choose our response.

"That gap between the stimulus that life brings and our response to that stimulus, our choices, is the world of character. The moral muscle we call character grows or shrinks in the crucible of our choices every day."

I added, "My wife tells me that we make literally hundreds of character choices every day. Being respectful or disrespectful, patient or impatient, kind or unkind, humble or arrogant, honest or dishonest. As creatures of habit, our choices soon become our habits. As my wife puts it, there are no human beings, only human becomings."

The teacher liked it. "Your wife is a wise woman, John. But never forget, my friends, that while we are free to make choices, we are not free to choose the consequences of our choices. The people we lead, those entrusted to our care, have to live with the consequences of our choices."

On cue, the principal had a quote. "A wise sage once said that our thoughts become our actions, our actions become our habits, our habits become our character, and our character becomes our destiny."

The planets and stars were aligning for the nurse. "I see it now. These things we have been discussing—like power, authority, serving, love, leadership—these things are all about our character. Even the qualities of love, like patience, kindness, humility, respectfulness, honesty, and commitment, are all acts of the will, that is, choices that forge our character."

"Yes, Kim," the teacher agreed. "The world is in dire need of leaders of character who serve their people by identifying and meeting their needs and helping them grow. By serving with character, leaders influence their people to action and inspire them to excellence."

Simeon was speaking Greg's language. "Couldn't agree more. I am now convinced that the vast majority of people

The Culture

are attracted to leaders of character and excellence. When leaders are operating in that zone, people want to be a part of it. If you are a person of character who creates excellence, people become motivated to raise their game."

Predictably, the preacher just had to disagree. "Not true, sarge. As a military man, you should know better than anyone that people are only motivated by carrots or sticks."

The sergeant remained cool yet assertive. "I disagree, sir. You don't motivate people by bribing or kicking them. You may get some brief activity using sticks and carrots, but you have in no way motivated that person."

"Can you support that?" the preacher challenged.

The sergeant thought for a moment. "Let me see if I can illustrate this principle for you, sir.

"My wife bought an ugly little poodle a few years ago, and he decided to make his home in my favorite chair. I decided I needed to motivate that dog to make a different choice.

"I began by utilizing the stick approach so the dog would know who was in charge. I rolled up my newspaper and gave that dog a little thump on the rear end. Of course, the poodle obediently jumped out of my chair."

The preacher yelled out, "Bingo! You motivated the dog."

"No, sir. What I got was some activity, a flurry of fluff as the dog exited my chair. Where do you think that dog was as soon as I left the room? Right back in my chair. Who was the only one in the room motivated? Me! The dog did not want to be out of my chair; *I* wanted the dog out of my chair.

"Now stay with me on this. My wife threatened to leave me if I continued to swat this dog, so I decided I needed to use more enlightened techniques—carrots. When the dog was in my chair, I would go to the kitchen and get a doggy treat to wave in his face. Guess what happened? The

Chapter Twelve: Character

dog obediently jumped out of my chair. Did I motivate the dog now?"

"It appears you did," the nurse responded.

"Things are not always as they appear, Kim. Yes, I again got some activity, but where do you think that dog was as soon as I went to work? Right back in my chair. The only one motivated in the room was me; I wanted that dog out of my chair. The dog still wanted to be in my chair.

"Lee, we cannot begin to talk about motivation in dogs, let alone human beings, until we understand motivation is about getting the fire going *within* someone. You don't have to be there to bribe or kick them. They would never let their team, the mission, or their leader down. Motivation is not lighting a fire under their butt; it is lighting a fire in their gut. They want to do it now."

The preacher grumbled something unintelligible.

"Greg is making a crucial point," the teacher added. "We now know that true motivation in human beings is the fruit of great leadership, character, excellence, mission, shared purpose, involvement, and community."

To me, the logic behind all of this was obvious, even self-evident.

We again sat in silence, but this time, I allowed myself to enter into the silence.

What was there to disagree with?

Out of the silence, a thought popped into my head, which I immediately shared.

"I am not good at putting things into words, but I think character needs to be in our definition of leadership."

Heads were nodding, so the teacher approached the whiteboard with our original leadership definition and rewrote it:

Leadership Defined:

The skill of influencing people to action with character that inspires confidence & excellence.

Chapter Thirteen

CHAOS

People need to be reminded more often than they need to be instructed.

Samuel Johnson

It was late afternoon, and the teacher stood gazing at the now-full white board containing our thoughts on leadership.

Leadership

= Awesome Responsibility
= Skill
≠ Power
= Authority (Influence)
= Serving
= Coaching (Hugging & Spanking)
= Character

Simeon turned and announced, "On behalf of the Gang of Seven, I present to you the seven essential principles of great leadership."

Everyone but the preacher rose to their feet and applauded.

As soon as we were seated, the coach blurted out, "I believe I just had an epiphany!"

"What on earth is an epiphany?" I cluelessly inquired.

The preacher hit me again. "Hey, fella, you might know if you went to church once in a while."

Before I could react, Theresa had already looked it up. "An epiphany is a sudden realization about the nature or meaning of something."

"Chris, please share your 'sudden realization' with us!" I teased, mostly to get my attention off the preacher.

The coach took a few moments to gather her thoughts. "Leadership is simply doing the right thing with the people we lead. Being patient, kind, appreciative, respectful, and humble are the right things to do. It is the right thing to do to be honest, to tell people the truth, and hold them accountable for their actions. It is the right thing to do to be committed to excellence and continuous improvement, and to inspire your team to be the best they can be.

"So, leadership is just doing the right thing. Character is doing the right thing. Like Greg said, leadership is simply character in action.

"I am dumbstruck by how simple and self-evident these leadership truths are. Why didn't I see it before?"

"Self-evident?" the principal asked? "How so?"

"Think about it, Theresa. Can you imagine someone saying they preferred a leader who was impatient, unkind, arrogant, disrespectful, selfish, unforgiving, dishonest, and uncommitted? Who would want to follow a leader like that?"

Chapter Thirteen: Chaos

After a few moments of silence, the nurse suddenly declared, "I'm feeling angry," although she didn't look or sound all that angry to me.

She continued. "I mean, what the heck, Simeon! We discussed many of these truths two years ago, and what good did it do? When you asked us who'd had a sustainable change in their lives, only Greg raised his hand.

"What's the point of all of this talking and training if we don't actually change? Why, after two years, was only one person able to make a sustainable change in their life?"

Hearing Kim articulate my deepest frustration was therapeutic and liberating for me. I was excited about what might come next.

Unfortunately, the preacher opened his mouth.

"I couldn't disagree more. I'm doing just fine as a leader. The only reason I didn't raise my hand yesterday was because I thought the question was silly. In addition, I must say I am finding myself pretty bored with this leadership review. I think I'm ready to move on to more advanced lessons on the subject."

That did it. The preacher pushed my final button.

"Are you kidding me? You really believe you get it? You have been rude and condescending all day and acting like a complete know-it-all. And now you want to move on to higher levels? Give me a break. You're clueless, man. And you call yourself a pastor?"

"What's your problem?" Lee shot back. "Just because *your* life is falling apart doesn't mean you have to project your issues all over *me*."

"Listen, my friend—" I responded.

The preacher cut me off mid-sentence. "I am not your friend."

That caught me off guard, but I quickly regained my bearings and continued, now shouting. "If you're not

89

interested in being here, why don't you just go back to the shallow, religious world you came from and spare us your negativity. We are all sick and tired of you and your snide comments."

"That's not how I feel," the teacher suddenly interjected. "Speak in the first person, John. Please don't assume you are speaking for the rest of us."

That hurt.

The nurse rushed in to rescue. "I think everyone needs to settle down. This is getting uncomfortable."

The preacher's face was beet red as he stood up. "I'm not going to take this crap. I don't need this." With that, he threw his belongings into his briefcase and stormed out of the room.

We sat in silence for several minutes until we heard a vehicle starting in the parking lot, followed by the sounds of flying gravel as the preacher made his noisy exit.

Most of the group looked shocked and dismayed.

To be honest, I felt pretty darn good about it.

"What was that all about?" I asked no one in particular, leaning back into my chair and throwing my legs up on the nearby ottoman.

Judging from the icy stares directed my way, I quickly deduced the group was not happy with me.

The teacher spoke first. "I am sorry Lee has chosen to leave us, but I cannot say I'm surprised. This has been building all day, and I'm disappointed the group has chosen to ignore the obvious dynamics. Now we are left with this unfortunate outcome."

"What could we have done, Simeon?" the nurse asked sheepishly.

"Healthy groups do not ignore obvious dysfunctional symptoms. Rather they take responsibility for the success and safety of the group—"

Chapter Thirteen: Chaos

"I couldn't take any more," I interrupted, trying my best to sound humble and hurt. "He just pushed my buttons."

The teacher was not having any of it. "He may have pushed *your* buttons, John, but they are your buttons for which you alone are responsible. You are also responsible for the choices you made in how you responded to Lee."

"Why did you have to raise your voice like that?" the nurse asked accusingly, like I had committed a crime or something.

"Kim," I responded defensively, "sometimes you have to let it rip to get people's attention and let them know they've crossed the line. Don't you agree, Simeon?"

"I do not agree, John," the teacher replied, stinging me again. "I can still remember the few times in my career where I lost my composure with a subordinate. I always believed that if I had to yell or get angry with someone to make my point, I was out of control. After all, I had all the power as the boss. I was dealing with adult professionals who were free to leave. Why did I need to shout? So I could feel better?"

The sergeant added, "In the past, I regularly went off on people because I thought that was the best way to make my point and confirm who was in charge. And it did make me feel better to blow off steam and get it off my chest. But what did my people get out of it? Anger and resentment. So once again, I was serving myself and not my people."

The coach coached me. "John, remember our discussion about gaps earlier today? In your mind, you had a standard of behavior, and you compared Lee's behavior against that standard, which created a gap. If you had gaps with Lee that needed to be discussed, that certainly didn't need to be an emotional or damaging event like we just witnessed."

Even the principal piled it on. "John, your comments were mean and a big withdrawal out of my relational account with you. It makes me feel like I can't trust you. Would you go off on me like that if I did something wrong?"

"So tell me what you all *really* think," I said angrily.

The crickets began chirping again.

Why was everyone ganging up on me?

Why was nobody defending me?

Why was I even here?

My impulse was to storm out of the room and make a scene just like the preacher had done.

The stimulus had arrived.

I now had to choose my response.

To this day, I thank God I made the right choice.

Chapter Fourteen

THE GIFT

*When the student is ready,
the teacher will appear.*

Ancient Proverb

It was a rough ending to a roller-coaster day.

At dinner, I chose to eat alone in the corner of the dining commons area. The group urged me to join them, but I chose to pout instead. The silent treatment was an old passive-aggressive behavior I utilized often to try to manipulate others.

After dinner, I sneaked back to my room to hide. I decided to phone my wife, even though I dreaded the thought of the usual arguing and tension.

And then it hit me. An epiphany? Why not change my response when the inevitable stimulus arrived? I made a silent resolution to really listen with an intent to understand rather than with an intent to reply or argue. I resolved to not get hooked when the button pushing began.

Rachael answered her cell phone without even saying hello. She matter-of-factly reported that our son had been suspended for playing a pornographic video game in school and a parental meeting with school administration officials was scheduled for Tuesday morning.

She proceeded to lecture me about my incompetence and failings as a father and husband and ended by asking me when I planned to get in the game.

In short, nearly every button on my psychic dashboard was pushed in under thirty seconds.

But they were, as the teacher had said, *my* buttons.

Miraculously, I chose to stick to my commitment and did not react. Rather, I listened closely and made efforts to understand Rachael's feelings rather than thinking about my response.

Failing to get a reaction, Rachael tried to hook me on a couple of other issues, but I refused to bite. My response, or lack thereof, caught her off guard.

The line went silent for a few moments before she asked, "Are you okay?"

I assured her I was fine and was looking forward to seeing her late Sunday night.

She fumbled for words before stammering, "Oh, well, okay then, see you tomorrow night. Goodbye, John."

I could tell Rachael sensed a change. She may have thought I had finally decided to take the "mellow meds" she and her doctor friend had failed to get me to try. Whatever she thought, I knew she sensed our dance was changing.

Unfortunately, I laid awake the entire night, ruminating. My only company and sole distraction was a small spider methodically weaving an intricate web around the simple light fixture above my bed.

Chapter Fourteen: The Gift

Sunday morning finally arrived, and I shuffled into class feeling tired and depressed. Probably sensing my misery, everyone mercifully avoided verbal or eye contact with me.

Of course, Simeon was full of life and energy. "Good morning! As I elaborated upon yesterday, my life experiences have convinced me that the very best organizations of two or more people gathered together for a purpose have something in common. They have successfully created a culture of excellence and sustained it over time. I have yet to see an exception.

"And I promise you a culture of excellence does not happen by merely showing up. A great culture is not some organic phenomenon that just happens. Indeed, the only thing you can count on to happen organically is a culture of mediocrity. To reiterate, my belief is that creating a culture of excellence requires a committed, intentional effort to grow leaders and build community.

"To illustrate this principle, I would like to share a true story with you."

I half-expected a sarcastic comment or challenge from the preacher before remembering he was no longer in our midst. The thought brought a smile to my lips.

The teacher continued. "The story concerns the near collapse and dissolution of this monastery, St. John of the Cross, nearly a century ago."

The principal was surprised. "Wow, St. John of the Cross is one the most successful and thriving monasteries in the United States, if not the world, today. You guys nearly went under?"

"We did. This monastic order was founded by Swiss monks in the Benedictine tradition, a decade prior to the Civil War. The monastery thrived with great leadership and community until the end of the World War I, when a gradual deterioration of the founding principles occurred.

"In fact, by the mid-1920s, all that remained was the abbot, their leader, and less than a dozen others, all over 75 years of age. St. John of the Cross was a dying organization.

"Now, not far from here lived an old rabbi from the local synagogue who was known throughout the region as a man of great wisdom. One day, following morning prayers, the abbot decided to visit the rabbi and ask him if he might offer a few words of wisdom that might help him to save his dying monastery.

"Unfortunately, the old rabbi could not help. He merely sympathized with the abbot, lamenting that he was experiencing similar problems in his own sphere of influence.

"The rabbi and the abbot spent time discussing the spiritual decline of the times, a period we now remember as the roaring 20s. Both were deeply troubled by what the future might hold.

"As the abbot was leaving, he pleaded with the rabbi to give him something, a tidbit, a sliver of wisdom that might help him save his dying monastery.

"The rabbi was silent for a few moments before saying, 'There really is only one thing you and your brothers at the monastery need to know.'

"The desperate abbot lit up. 'Really? One thing? Please, tell me what it is.'"

"The old rabbi looked deeply into the abbot's eyes. 'One of you is the Messiah.'

"Confused by the rabbi's advice, the abbot returned to the monastery where his brothers were eagerly awaiting the outcome of the visit.

"'He really wasn't much help,' the abbot sadly replied. 'However, he did mention a rather peculiar thing as I was leaving. He told me that the Messiah is one of us. I do not know what he meant.'"

"Now, in the weeks that followed, the old monks spent

Chapter Fourteen: The Gift

a great deal of time pondering the rabbi's words.

"'The Messiah is one of us? What is that supposed to mean? Is the rabbi just an old, senile Jew trying to insult us? After all, we believe the Messiah has already come. Or is there something deeper? Is there something we're missing?'

"More time passed and the monks could not shake the nagging notion that there might be some significance to the rabbi's words.

"'The Messiah is one of us? Do you think he meant one of us here at the monastery? If so, which one?'

"'Maybe it's our abbot. Yes, that would make sense, as he has been our leader for nearly a generation.

"'But what about Brother Luke? He is a devout man of the spirit, and one of our longest residents. On the other hand, Luke is getting a bit forgetful and is pretty high maintenance these days. Luke couldn't be the Messiah, could he?'

"'Or perhaps Brother Matthew? He has been here over thirty years, although he nearly renounced his vows years ago over a woman he met at a retreat. Scandalous! Then again, since that episode, there is no brother more committed than Matthew. And he possesses great wisdom. Could Matthew be the Messiah?'

"'How about Brother Thomas? Impossible. His uniqueness is his uncanny ability to irritate others. Yet Thomas does have a way of being there when you need him. When the going gets tough, Thomas is right by your side. Could Thomas be the dark-horse Messiah?'

"'And what about me? Could I be the Messiah? At least that's an easy call. I'm certainly no Messiah!'

"More time passed and the monks continued to wrestle with the rabbi's words. But as they did, they began to treat each other with a new respect and deeper kindness, perhaps as insurance against one of them actually being the Messiah. And on the remote chance that each monk himself might be the Messiah, they began to treat themselves with greater respect and kindness.

"Now, the grounds surrounding the monastery at that time were as amazing and beautiful as they are today. Consequently, people from throughout the region still came to visit, to picnic, to meditate, and to pray.

"Before long, the visitors began to notice a change. It was subtle at first, but they began to sense something unique and distinctive. There was an aura of extraordinary respect that now began to surround the old monks and seemed to permeate the atmosphere of the monastery. They couldn't quite place their finger on what it was, but there was something mystically attractive, even compelling, that inexorably drew them back.

"They began to bring their families and friends to show them this special place and their friends brought their friends. Before long, the monastery had a steady flow of visitors from around the region and beyond.

"And then it happened.

"One of the younger visitors asked the abbot if he could join the monastery. Soon after, another asked. And then another. And another.

"Within a few years, our dying community had once again become a thriving monastic order.

"Thanks to the rabbi's gift."

Chapter Fifteen

ENVIRONMENT

*Men and women want to do a good job.
If they are provided a proper environment, they will do so.*

Bill Hewlett
Founder, Hewlett-Packard

"I loved it!" the nurse gushed. "Thank you for sharing your story with us, Simeon."

The sergeant seconded, "Yes, sir, lots of great takeaways."

The teacher looked pleased. "I am so happy you found value in a chapter from our history. Let's take a few minutes and discuss the lessons we can learn from our past."

The coach was ready. "What jumped out at me was how clueless the monks were. Here they were, living in a religious institution, and yet lacking love and respect toward one another, let alone the outside world.

"I guess you could say that they knew about love, but didn't know love. Like what we talked about yesterday where you can know about something and not really know it."

I added, "I was struck by how they had been slowly dying for years, and yet were unable or unwilling to face their predicament until nearly the end. I think we easily become blinded to what is happening right before our eyes. Maybe that's why shrinks and consultants are so busy. We sometimes need help from the outside to better see our stuff. Kudos to the abbot for finally reaching out for help."

The principal agreed. "Not only did the abbot reach out for help, he reached out to a somewhat hostile source. By that, I mean he sought the help of someone whose theology and worldview were very different from his own. That's hard to do. It's far easier to discount or write off people we don't agree with or like. Powerful lessons can come from strange places.

"And I give the other monks a lot of credit as well. They were willing to bear the trial of being uncomfortable and having their paradigms challenged in the hopes that new truths might be discovered. Evidently, their persistence was rewarded."

"Yes, Theresa," the nurse added, "but the monks still had to do their own work. They had to do their own changing."

"So true," the principal agreed. "Leo Tolstoy said everyone wants to change the world, but nobody wants to change themselves. And Alcoholics Anonymous wisely teaches that the only person you can change is yourself. We have to do our own changing, just like we have to do our own dying."

"Great points, ladies," the sergeant joined in. "Each monk had to do their part, become a group of all leaders like we discussed earlier. The abbot was still their formal leader, but each monk had to step up and take responsibility for the failures of the past as well as the solutions for the future."

Greg's remarks reminded me of something. "I have often heard my wife speak of the first rule of group dynamics, which is, if you are part of a dysfunctional team, you are part of the problem. She tells me that people do not take kindly to hearing those words."

The principal was looking guilty. "Years ago, at work, I got called on that very thing.

"Back in my teaching days, I worked for a crazy principal whom the teachers affectionately referred to as the "bosshole." I mentioned him earlier. I would just shut down in the presence of this jerk. I'd sit in meetings and nod in agreement with everything, and never challenge a thing he said. But after the meeting, I would slam him and his ideas to anyone who would listen.

"Eventually, a colleague pointed out to me that I was part of the problem, and contributing to our dysfunctional team.

"I nearly lost it. How could she suggest I was part of the problem when everyone could clearly see who the problem was?

"She told me that my silence and refusal to challenge was enabling his behavior, and my duplicitous backstabbing was sabotaging the spirit of the team. In addition, my silence was a refusal to participate in finding a solution and a failure to take responsibility for our team. She told me that once I stopped participating, I had lost my right to be a critic.

"Her comments hurt, and I was mad at her for a while, but once I got over it, I saw the wisdom in what she was saying. My attitude of 'Not my circus, not my monkeys' was contributing to the group's dysfunction.

"So, I started to speak up in meetings and began challenging that old geezer. I learned that bullies usually back down when others push back, which is, in actuality, what they need. It was a risk, but over time, he came to respect me, and we actually became friends. And the team began functioning at a higher level. None of that would have happened had I not made the choice to accept responsibility for our team."

Simeon looked pleased. "Great points. Anybody else?"

"Love is contagious," came the soft reply from the nurse. "I was struck by how the monks were initially critical of one another until they began to look deeper. Once they got past the superficial things, they began to find the good in each other. We all need to look a little deeper."

"Exactly, Kim," the coach agreed. "I think they call it selective perception. We find what we're looking for. When the monks were looking for defects and issues with one another, they found them. When they changed their filter, and began looking for the good in one another, they found that as well."

The principal concurred. "Yes, and selective perception is contagious and habit forming. In the many different school districts and buildings I have worked in over the years, I am amazed by how contagious a negative culture can be.

"But the reverse is also true. A culture that values catching people doing things right, being positive, kind and exhibiting loving behaviors toward others is also contagious.

"As creatures of habit, we can easily get caught up and changed by the dynamics of the environment we are in, which is why we need to be careful where we spend our time."

Silence descended upon the group.

"What about you, Simeon?" the sergeant inquired. "What is your takeaway from the experience of your predecessors?"

"Thank you for asking, Greg. Whenever I tell that story, I am reminded of the movie, *Field of Dreams*."

"That's one of my all-time favorite movies!" I practically shouted. "If you build it, they will come."

Chapter Fifteen: Environment

The teacher continued. "For me, this is the essence of it and sums up what was experienced here many years ago: Creating and sustaining an environment or culture of excellence requires commitment and effort. My predecessors got sloppy and lost their way; but thankfully, they recovered.

"If you build something great, then great people will be attracted to it. It's the Law of the Harvest: You reap what you sow. If you sow a safe, healthy environment where excellence is the standard, you will reap a thriving culture and great people will come. Great customers, employees, shareholders, vendors, and other key stakeholders will come, and they will stay. Excellence in leadership and community is compelling and contagious."

The coach jumped in. "Nature shows us this truth in spades. I love to garden, but the truth is that I cannot make anything grow. God only knows why a tiny seed becomes a large tree that bears fruit.

"But what I *can* do is create the environment that will make it possible for the fruit to come. If I prepare the soil, water, fertilize, weed, and make sure it gets sunshine, I can trust the fruit will come."

"This is also true with human beings," the nurse added. "Conditions in the womb must be perfect for a thriving baby to be born. Once born, babies must be nurtured and loved, or they do not develop properly."

The principal frowned. "Amen to that, sister. We see the results of young people growing up in unhealthy environments every day in our schools. I think you will find more of the same in our overcrowded prisons. Wouldn't it be nice if we nurtured our kids in the high chair rather than letting the state punish them in the electric chair?"

The nurse had more. "In my profession, people often feel that they are going to a doctor to be healed, but that is incorrect. Medical professionals do not heal anyone. What

The Culture

we do is create the necessary conditions and environment for the body to heal itself."

I could relate. "My wife, the shrink, has often said that young therapists mistakenly believe they can fix, change, or heal people. With experience, they come to understand that the best they can do is create the right conditions, a safe and therapeutic environment where people can begin to grow and heal."

The teacher summarized. "Great examples! And this is why creating a healthy culture is so crucial in any organization of two or more people gathered together for a purpose. If you place normal human beings in a healthy environment, then good fruit will be produced. An abundant harvest of good, long-lasting fruit will simply not appear in toxic or dysfunctional environments.

"The good news is that we have the technology, the know-how, to create a culture of excellence by growing leaders and building community. It's been around for centuries.

"The bad news is that you must be willing to do the work of applying the principles because there are no short cuts and there is no magic dust. You must be willing to grow and change."

The nurse frowned. "But I don't like change! Other than a wet baby, who likes change?"

For the morning break, I found a bench overlooking the lake and sat alone reflecting on the morning lessons.

Before long, I heard, and then saw, a vehicle quickly approaching the monastery up the two-track trail.

"Who on earth could that be?" I mumbled as I watched the speeding truck approach, followed by a large, rising plume of sand, dirt, and dust.

The vehicle was moving recklessly fast as it swerved into the parking lot close to where I was sitting. The driver slammed on the brakes, sending rocks and sand flying in every direction, including on me, which instantly ticked me off.

As the cloud cleared, the driver climbed hastily out of the truck and headed right toward me.

I could not believe my eyes.

It was the preacher.

Chapter Sixteen

FAKING

The worst crime is faking it.

Kurt Cobain

I was tongue-tied as the preacher approached, but it didn't matter because he stomped right past me.

Since our session was about to resume, I followed the preacher into the classroom, maintaining a safe distance. There was an awkward tension in the room as all eyes followed him to his seat. No one uttered a word.

Predictably, and to my dismay, the teacher sincerely and warmly welcomed him. "I am so glad you are back, Lee."

The preacher mumbled some unintelligible words.

The teacher pushed a little more. "Would you like to talk about what happened?"

"No, sir. Let's just move along. Please."

The teacher paused, probably hoping one of us might welcome him, but all eyes were fixed on the floor or ceiling.

Simeon chose to move forward. "Our agreed-upon goal this weekend is to gain insight into creating a culture of excellence wherever we lead by growing leaders and building high-performing teams. We also agreed to explore the steps necessary to making real and sustainable changes in our lives.

"Yesterday, we spent time reviewing the qualities of great leadership. We will now turn our attention to defining the qualities of high-performing teams, what I refer to as 'community.' Later today, the rubber will meet the road as we explore personal change and the steps necessary for growing leaders and building community in the real world."

The principal was excited. "I've been looking forward to this. But first, we need to clarify our terms. Please define high-performing teams and community."

The teacher smiled. "My pleasure, Theresa. I see high-performing teams and community as synonymous. But whatever words you use to label it, I am referring to a group of two or more people who are committed to creating excellence together.

"It's a team that is committed to creating a healthy and psychologically safe environment that allows group members to focus on the mission and pursue excellence as free as possible from the political nonsense and bad behaviors that derail so many teams.

"It's a place where members are growing as leaders and learning to take responsibility for the success of their team. Where members are learning to accept and transcend their differences, resolve conflict rather than avoid it, disarm themselves of their personal barriers, and communicate effectively by practicing assertiveness and active listening.

"Forgive me for rambling, but a community or high-performing team is all of those things to me."

"Sounds heavenly, Simeon," I cynically interjected. "But is creating a place like that even possible in the real world?"

Chapter Sixteen: Faking

"Not only is it possible, John, but I have experienced it many times in my work and personal life. The catch is that you have to be willing to do the work required because community does not happen by accident, except for short periods of time in response to a crisis. We will discuss that later.

"The work of building community, trust, and emotional connections between people requires commitment combined with intentional efforts. But the fruits of those efforts are enormous."

I felt myself inwardly cringe when the preacher began to speak, but then relaxed a little when I immediately noticed less attitude in his voice. "Simeon, how would you go about creating a place like that?"

The teacher smiled. "Glad you asked, Lee. To better grasp the team or community-building process, I think it is helpful to first describe the stages that groups typically travel through on their way to achieving community or high performance. There are four."

The coach excitedly jumped in. "Forming, storming, norming, and performing! Is that correct, Simeon?

"I know about this because just last month I completed a teambuilding clinic put on by the NCAA. We learned there are many different names for these four stages, but the dynamics of each stage have been identified and understood for many decades. As I recall, one model referred to the stages as pseudo-community, chaos, emptying, and community. Yet another model labeled the stages as polite, bid for power, constructive, and esprit."

The teacher clapped. "Bravo, Chris! You learned well.

"For our purposes, I would like to refer to the stages of team development as the four F's: faking, fighting, forming, and functioning. For me, these labels more accurately describe what is happening during each particular stage."

The sergeant repeated, "Faking, fighting, forming and functioning, the four F's. Okay, Simeon, I'll try to stay with you, but this is new ground for me. What's this faking stage all about?"

"Faking is the pretending or pseudo-community stage, the stage when members pretend they are a team and a close-knit group but in reality are not. They talk superficially and avoid expressing differences in opinions or worldviews. The unwritten rules in this stage are to make a good impression, be nice, and above all, don't rock the boat.

"In the beginning, this pretending stage can be innocent and harmless. But over time, this pretense and superficiality has a dark side as members avoid talking about uncomfortable topics or areas of disagreement that may be crucial for the health and even the survival of the group."

"Examples please?" the principal insisted.

The teacher was ready. "Examples of the faking stage could include the courtship period for couples, the early days on a new job, the first day of class, meeting new people, and social settings like cocktail parties.

"Everyone is cordial and sweet. 'How are you?' 'Fine.' 'How are you?' 'Fine.' 'It rained today.' 'Yes, it is wet out.' 'Why yes, it is wet.' And on it goes. It is the dance of superficial niceties."

The nurse asked, "Simeon, other than the sweet talk, how is one able to identify or diagnose if they are in this faking stage?"

"There are at least three more symptoms that I am aware of, Kim: avoiding conflict, speaking in generalities, and boredom.

"Avoiding conflict is a dead giveaway for the faking stage, as members will go to great lengths to avoid uncomfortable topics. It's as if everyone is operating according to the rules that any good hostess knows. Don't talk about politics, religion, or anything people might disagree with. If anyone says something that challenges the status quo or offends sensibilities, quickly change the subject, pretend nothing happened, and move on."

I moaned. "Sounds like many of the gatherings I've attended over the years."

"Or business meetings," the preacher added, getting more involved now. "Just be nice, don't rock the boat, and get along."

"Or," the principal added, "going to places like church and getting hugged and kissed by people I don't even know. Drives me nuts. It's like, 'Do I know you?' I hate it when people pretend we have built a relationship when we clearly have not."

"What about the boredom thing?" the coach asked.

"People in the faking stage are generally bored stiff. Examples include cocktail parties, business meetings, holidays with relatives, many marriages, and lots of religious institutions across the land. I am sad to say that many of our mainline denominational churches in America are dying, and I'm convinced a primary reason is because people are so bored. A fake community has little life in it."

The coach pushed for more. "What about speaking in generalities?"

"People in the faking stage often speak in broad terms using stereotypical anecdotes. Group members let them get away with this, even though on the inside they may vehemently disagree."

"Examples, please?" the principal asked.

I had one. "Cocktail parties are full of that kind of behavior, which is why I hate them so much. Someone says, 'Oh, divorce is a terrible thing,' or 'Our parents did the best they could,' and everyone politely agrees as if the wisdom of the ages has been spoken.

"But I can assure you that someone is probably thinking, 'My divorce was the best thing that ever happened to me,' or 'My father didn't do his best, I'm quite sure of that.'

"But they would never say it. That might get uncomfortable and require them to explain their position. It's far easier just to agree and move on."

"Or at work," the nurse jumped in. "Our head administrator often starts meetings by saying, 'We are certainly a strong, united team.' Every time I hear it, I want to vomit. I sit there and think, 'I have never been part of a more dysfunctional team in my twenty-five years in nursing.'

"But you know what? I don't say it. I just politely smile and nod my head. Yuck."

"Or at many religious places," the principal added, "everyone pretends they believe the same stuff, yet I know there are many different thoughts, ideas, theologies, and opinions. But it just isn't safe to express them.

"I was at a church meeting once, and a man got up and said, 'Just trust God, and all will be well.' And everyone nodded as if he had issued some universal decree.

"Yet, I know that there were people sitting in the meeting thinking, 'You know, I've tried that 'trust God' jazz, and it didn't work for me. I'm still struggling.'

"Of course, nobody says a word because if they did, they would probably get pounded with Bible verses and mini-sermons to get their thinking straight. It's much easier and safer just to agree."

"Wonderful examples!" the teacher exclaimed. "You've captured the essence of this faking stage.

"As we have said, the faking stage is boring, little gets accomplished, and there is no life in it. The good news is that this produces the necessary friction to push the group into the next stage.

"Yes! The fighting stage," the sergeant bellowed. "Back in the day, it was my personal favorite!"

Chapter Seventeen

FIGHTING

*I divorced my husband for religious reasons.
He thought he was God, and I didn't.*

Former wife

Something was bothering the coach.

"Before we move forward, I need to say something. I'm hesitant to speak because the group may not like what I have to say. But I feel moved to speak, so I think I probably should.

"I am convinced that our group is locked in stage one. We are essentially a shallow, pretend community and have been faking it all along."

"Why would you say that?" the principal lashed out, sounding offended.

"Because I believe it's true. We have sat here for two days without dealing with or barely acknowledging the dynamics going on within the group. That strikes me as phony."

"Well, that's just your opinion," the principal shot back.

The coach refused to budge. "Theresa, the difference between fact and opinion is the presence of evidence. There is a lot of evidence to support my statement."

The principal wasn't budging either. "Like?"

"Yesterday morning when we reintroduced ourselves, only Simeon shared deeply, while most of us gave little more than superficial details.

"Then John shared deeply, offering up some of his brokenness, and not one of us acknowledged his pain. Nobody wanted to go there, even with Simeon prodding us.

"We also sat here watching Lee and John go at it, and nobody said a word except to change the subject. Simeon even tried to get us to discuss Lee leaving our group, and again when he returned, but we refused.

"I think we know a little about each other but really don't know each other at all."

Theresa didn't like it. "Well, we just don't agree with that."

"Theresa, what do you mean by 'we?'" the sergeant asked, also sounding offended. "Please speak in the first person because I, for one, believe Chris is absolutely correct. What has been going on here is pretty abnormal."

"I agree with Theresa," the nurse chimed in. "How about you, John, whose side are you on?"

Not wanting to get sucked in, I just stared at the floor.

The crickets returned. The tension in the room was palpable.

Suddenly, guttural sounds could be heard coming from the preacher's direction, and I glanced his way. His entire body was shaking, and he was sobbing uncontrollably. He looked like a crushed man.

Through his veil of tears, he suddenly blurted out a confession. "I want each of you to know how very sorry

I am for being such a jerk this weekend. The truth is, my life is a disaster, and I'm a total wreck these days. I hope you will forgive me."

———∞∞∞———

With the preacher's unexpected display of brokenness and vulnerability, my anger and resentment toward him dissipated like air from a balloon. To my surprise, I even reached over and patted his arm. In a strange way, I even began to experience a bit of his pain.

The guy obviously had issues, but who was I to judge and write him off as a loser? My own life was pretty much a train wreck on all fronts, including being considered a jerk by most who knew me.

My wife often lectured me about lacking empathy for others, which I never really understood and wrote off as psycho-babble. I'm pretty sure I was experiencing that empathy thing for the very first time.

———∞∞∞———

The group sat in awkward silence.

After a while, the teacher moved us forward. "Is there anything else that needs to be said?"

More silence.

The teacher surprised us all by declaring, "I am so proud of you! Things are beginning to get real in here. And I believe we will gain further insight into our group's dynamics as we move forward and discuss the next stage of group development. Would that be okay?"

We all quickly nodded. Anything was better than this.

"As mentioned earlier, the faking stage is boring and

unproductive, which can create the necessary friction to propel the group into the second stage."

"The storming or fighting stage," the nurse reminded us. "In my team-building class, I was intrigued by this stage, even though I hate conflict. This is the stage when the pretense and faking passes away and the masks are lowered."

"The honeymoon is over," the preacher suggested, still wiping away tears. "Suddenly you're having disagreements with your new spouse, boss, or co-workers. We thought we were destined for eternal bliss but soon discover our teammates are different than we are, and their behaviors and quirks can get under our skin. I hate it when that happens!"

The coach laughed. "So true, Lee. In my work life, I had jobs where everybody was sweet and cordial the first few days, but before long, they were looking at me saying, 'Do I know you?' The courtship—or pretense, as Kim called it—doesn't last long."

The teacher nodded. "In this stage, the pleasantries and small talk have passed, the masks are dropped, and individual differences and agendas are now getting exposed. Group members begin to act out in various ways, including displaying behaviors or personal barriers that damage relationships and trust. We will spend more time discussing these personal barriers in a minute.

"However, disagreement or struggle alone is not determinative of stage two. Indeed, there is often disagreement and tension in a healthy group operating in true community.

"The key difference in this stage is that the fighting is unproductive, chaotic, and heading nowhere. Little gets resolved as members swat back and forth at one other with little effort to listen, understand, or empathize with other points of view. In this stage, people just want their way."

"Sounds like my first marriage," the principal said. "Not long after our wedding vows and honeymoon, the beast emerged. It was his way or the highway. I suffered through two bosses at work just like him."

The teacher continued. "As individual differences and personal barriers emerge in this fighting or storming stage, group members often transform into little dictators, amateur MBAs, psychologists, PhDs, and preachers. They hammer others with their agendas, opinions, world views, and dogmas as they attempt to control, change, fix, or convert others to their point of view.

"People often believe they are genuinely helping others to see the light, but in reality, stage two behavior is often self-centered and self-serving."

"How so, Simeon?" the sergeant asked.

"If your thoughts, opinions, or ways of doing things are different from mine, it calls my ideas and methods into question, which is challenging and uncomfortable for me. After all, I've worked hard for what I believe and how I operate. And I may not take kindly to working through or rethinking my position because, heck, that would take a lot of effort.

"On the other hand, if I can convert or change you to my way of thinking, I get to be the hero by fixing you, as well as being the smartest person in the room. Isn't that awesome? How much easier and nicer that would be than extending myself to understand you and where you're coming from."

"No wonder it's called the chaos or fighting stage," Theresa observed. "When people try to change, fix, or dump their stuff on me, my first reaction is to push back. I mean, who appointed you my personal guru or messiah? Maybe you should mind your own business. I can definitely see how this stage would push people's buttons."

The coach was intrigued. "Well put. I learned in my recent clinic that these two stages are built upon lies. Unconscious, perhaps, but lies nevertheless."

The nurse looked puzzled. "Lies? How so?"

"In the faking stage, members buy into the lie that differences between people are undesirable, even detrimental to building bonds and group cohesion. This false belief, or lie, convinces group members that they must be nice at all costs, which includes withholding the truth, avoiding conflict, and being less than honest about how they really feel.

"Yet, the premise is false. Our group strength often resides in our differences and our diversity. All of us together are much wiser than any one of us. When we learn to accept one another, and transcend our differences, that becomes the foundation for establishing tight bonds and emotional connections, which builds trust and unity."

The nurse pressed for more. "What about the lies in the fighting stage, Chris?"

"If I understand Simeon correctly, in this stage, our differences are now exposed. The lie is that we must fix, change, convert, silence, or eliminate people who don't see or do things our way.

"We even convince ourselves that fixing and changing others is in the best interests of the individual and the group, even if we have to resort to bad behavior. But the result of trying to change and fix others in this manner is often resentment, alienation, and damaged relationships, as Theresa just pointed out."

The coach was on a roll. "Another lie during this fighting stage is that members falsely believe the team is regressing, getting sick, becoming dysfunctional, degenerating, even dying.

"'We never fought like this before we were married,' or

Chapter Seventeen: Fighting

'We always had cordial, although dreary, business meetings until Ed joined the team and started challenging things,' or 'We always had nice, although often boring, Bible studies until Sarah started sharing her newfangled perspectives and theologies.'

"So, the lie is that our group is degenerating when the truth is that the group is finally starting to get healthy. It doesn't feel like it, but our feelings are often poor barometers of the truth."

"You're right, Chris," the nurse added, gaining insight. "The truth is that the chaos or fighting stage is actually healthier than the faking stage where we pretend we have no differences when we really do. Faking it is the biggest lie of all.

"At least in the fighting stage, the differences are exposed, and the masks have been removed. We have not yet learned to resolve our differences in a civil manner, but at least they are on the table, and we have an opportunity to move toward resolution and community together."

"Wonderful, wonderful!" the teacher exclaimed. "Now, to escape the chaos or fighting, it is common in this stage for members to attack the leader. 'We wouldn't be quarreling like this if we had good leadership,' they will snipe.

"Or, more commonly, dictators will forcefully emerge and simply order the group out of the chaos. 'I'm the boss, and this is the way it's going to be. It's my way or the highway.' Or, 'I'm the pastor here. From now on, I will decide what we believe.' Or, 'I'm the head of the house, and what I say goes.'"

The principal added, "But quashed dissent always seeks an outlet. As the old saying goes, you have not converted a person by silencing them."

"But it does stop the fighting and chaos," the nurse suggested.

"Perhaps, temporarily, Kim," the teacher agreed.

The Culture

"Ordering the group to cease and desist is certainly one way to control things. The downside is that the group will never become a high-performing team because dictatorship and community are mutually exclusive.

"The chaos may have ceased, but we have resolved nothing. We have not learned to listen, empathize, or compromise. We have not grown as individuals or as a team. We have only been silenced and sent to our corner. Until the next round.

"Sadly, the vast majority of groups, including marriages, spend their entire existence bouncing back and forth between these stages of faking and fighting. They never seem to break out of the dance."

"Fortunately, there is a way forward."

Chapter Eighteen

FORMING

*If everyone sweeps in front of their own door,
the whole street will be clean.*

Geothe

It was lunchtime, and for the first time, all seven of us walked to the dining room and broke bread together. No one even glanced at an electronic device.

Afterward, we sat in a circle in the main library, taking turns feeding pieces of dry birch into the gaping mouth of the giant stone fireplace.

And we talked. And listened.

And we talked some more.

Something had changed. The conversation had moved to a different level as people shared more honestly and deeply. Questions became more penetrating and answers more revealing. Greater efforts were made to understand

The Culture

differing viewpoints, yet quick and easy solutions were not carelessly offered. There was raucous laughter as well as deeply felt tears.

As the teacher had observed, it was starting to get real.

Two hours flew by before we gathered in the classroom for our final afternoon together.

"As I mentioned before lunch," the teacher began, "most groups never grow beyond the first two stages of development. They seem content to play group ping pong between faking and fighting and back again."

The coach could relate. "My first coaching position was in a private school where I worked for a real command-and-control whack job. There would be periods of relative peace, followed by utter chaos when a situation or individual challenged her. The whole staff would then walk on pins and needles, keeping their heads down until the next blow-up. I can't believe I stayed there as long as I did."

"That was my first marriage, I'm ashamed to say," lamented the principal. "There were regular and predictable bouts of raging and ultimatums followed by my silent treatment, which resulted in new jewelry to buy my compliance until the next round. An endless loop until I got out."

"There is another way," the teacher matter-of-factly announced. "The good news is that we have the know-how to build community. The bad news is—"

"We know," I said. "We have to be willing to change and do the work, right Simeon?"

No response was needed.

"Stage three, the forming stage, is when the true work of team formation and becoming a thriving community really begins.

"This is the stage when group members become aware of and begin to work on their personal agendas and/or bad behaviors, what I refer to as personal barriers. They stop their futile attempts to fix and change others and begin to look within themselves as a source of the problem. They start to truly listen and understand one another while letting go of their personal agendas and insatiable need to have things go their way.

"In short, this is the stage when group members begin to realize that if they are part of a dysfunctional team, they themselves are part of the problem. Sadly, most teams, including marriages, never get to this point. Any guesses on why?"

The words tumbled out of my mouth. "Because it's hard. It takes effort and humility to take a hard look at yourself, let alone do something about it. It takes little effort to point across the dinner or conference room table and tell others they are the problem. Believe me, I've done both my whole life."

The teacher nodded. "Precisely, John. What is required to move toward true community and high performance is for group members to begin to identify and overcome their personal barriers for the sake of the team and its mission."

"You keep mentioning personal barriers," came the principal's predictable query. "Please define."

The teacher obliged. "By personal barriers, I am referring to those undesirable behaviors and character defects that damage trust, cooperation, and relationships. These personal barriers stand in the way of the team reaching high performance and a sense of community.

"And here's the kicker: We all have personal barriers. In fact, if you don't believe you have personal barriers, that makes another one you can add to your list. Indeed, it may well be your worst barrier of all."

The Culture

"Interesting," the principal considered, rubbing her chin. "I need examples of these personal barriers."

"There are dozens. Barriers could include being rude, disrespectful, egotistical, failing to listen, avoiding conflict, failing to assume responsibility, failing to be authentic, being over-controlling or over-domineering, harboring prejudices, putting people in boxes, lacking assertiveness, backstabbing, and pairing. There are many others. In fact, I prepared a handout for you that lists many common barriers."[3]

We each took a copy and spent time looking it over. It was painful to see the many destructive behaviors I routinely engaged in.

"Simeon, how can we know for sure which barriers are ours?" the nurse wondered.

"Through personal reflection as well as candid and honest feedback from others. In a few minutes, we will discuss an effective feedback tool for uncovering personal barriers as well as for developing leaders.

"It's important to note that the necessary component in the forming stage is the willingness of group members to grow and change. As we said earlier, you cannot improve unless you change.

"Consequently, group members must be teachable, open to receiving honest feedback, and willing to sacrifice and surrender their personal barriers and agendas for the sake of the team. When these dynamics and choices happen within a group, magic arrives."

"And we call that magic 'community.'"

"Let me be sure I've got this," the coach said. "The bridge to community or high performance occurs when group members decide that the team and its mission is of greater importance than their habitual behaviors or personal agendas. Members then willingly choose to surrender or sacrifice

---

[3] This handout is included in Appendix A.

Chapter Eighteen: Forming

their personal barriers for a greater good, which is the welfare of the team and its mission."

The teacher was beaming. "That's the essence of it."

The nurse suddenly changed course. "We have a lot of personal barriers in this group."

"Please speak in the first person, Kim," the teacher encouraged. "It's an important principle of community building."

"Thank you for the reminder, Simeon. I have personal barriers that may be preventing this group from reaching community. I have avoided conflict by not speaking up when bad behavior was occurring. This is something I've been doing my whole life. I was a middle child and survived by making peace with everyone at all costs.

"I always rush in to rescue people from their bad behavior as you've seen me do this weekend. I see how this barrier has caused many of my relationship problems over the years, including my relationship with this group."

A thoughtful silence ensued. No one jumped in to rescue or fix her.

The sergeant spoke. "Don't think you've got a corner on the barrier market, Kim. I didn't say anything either, but for different reasons. I was actually enjoying it. How's that for messed up? It's probably why I became a drill sergeant; I love conflict. I have improved from two years ago, but I still have a long way to go."

I confessed next. "I have been told I do not suffer fools gladly."

"Are you calling me a fool?" the preacher reacted, but this time I'm pretty sure he was kidding.

"No. Of course not, Lee. What I mean is that I'm overly judgmental and quick to write people off for even small offenses. And once I have written someone off, it's nearly impossible for them to redeem themselves with me. I am

The Culture

finally seeing what my wife has been telling me for years, and it's a very ugly thing."

"Don't be too hard on yourself, partner," the preacher offered. "Here I am, a pastor, and my life is falling apart. Of course, I have never shared that with anyone because of my many barriers, including my fear of vulnerability and transparency. I'm scared to death of what people would think of me if they really knew me.

"Yet, I also know on a deeper level that without vulnerability and transparency, I will never have real community in my life. A pastor with no community. You think you folks have issues? I'll show you issues."

The coach jumped in. "Kim, how about John and I on the first morning break? We sat there, backstabbing Lee for his behavior, and Simeon as well for not providing better leadership in the group. Kim, you did the right thing by leaving our table."

"Perhaps, Chris," Kim replied. "But did you notice that I left you guys without explaining why I was uncomfortable? The assertive thing would have been to tell you both why I was leaving and ask you to take your issues directly to the source. But my barriers got in the way."

"Simeon," the principal said. "This 'personal barriers' sheet you gave us highlights backstabbing and pairing. Why is that, and would you please define these behaviors?"

"I'm so glad you asked, Theresa, because these are two of the most common, yet destructive, barriers of all. Simply put, backstabbing is having non-value-added discussions about people who are not in the room. Saying things about other people you probably would not say in their presence."

"I think we all get that one," Theresa responded.

"Pairing is a destructive alliance between two or more people. It's the same two or three who go to lunch or the bar together to talk about people in the group in a duplicitous way. Rather than talking to people directly about issues or problems, they break off and talk in little destructive huddles.

"Pairing and backstabbing are devastating to teams. In fact, in our Benedictine tradition, backstabbing and pairing are two of the few capital offenses that can get you kicked out of the monastery. We have learned from centuries of experience how destructive these behaviors are to community."

"All righty, then. Chris and I plead guilty," I confessed. "Please don't kick us out."

The confessions continued for the next ninety minutes. As the masks began to drop, the floodgates began to open, and community arrived.

One after another, people began to share deeply about the brokenness in their lives, including abusive childhoods, alcoholism, drug abuse, abortion, and failed marriages. I was blown away by what was shared. Turns out, I barely knew these people at all.

Paradoxically, there were many tears shed along with periods of out-of-control laughter. I laughed harder than I had in years, maybe ever. An outsider would have judged us to be a bipolar support group.

The sergeant called it our "opening the kimono" session, which got a laugh. Whatever it was, the authenticity, richness, and power of it rocked my world. I was tasting community for the first time.

I also had a stunning insight.

Underneath the masks of composure are wounded and hurting people.

Just like me.

I was not alone.

Chapter Nineteen

FUNCTIONING

*A player who makes a team great
is more valuable than a great player.*

Coach John Wooden

The teacher was delighted. "This sharing has made my year. I love the humility, vulnerability, and transparency. It gives me hope.

"Before we move to the fourth and final stage of group development, I want you to know that there is an exception to the stages we have discussed. It occurs when groups skip stages and quickly transform into high-functioning teams. Any thoughts on when this might occur?"

I knew the answer. "In response to a crisis. Early in my career, I was a young project manager working in a small, fifty-person, aluminum manufacturing firm. The company began to fail, and it became clear bankruptcy protection was imminent. Then, an amazing thing happened.

"The CEO got us all together and said we had to get

our act together if we were going to survive. He gave an inspiring speech about taking responsibility and pulling together for the good of the company and each other. Amazingly, we did.

"Overnight, it no longer mattered what your title was or whether you had a corner office. Everyone pulled together, office politics disappeared, and other jerky behavior ceased because survival was at stake. In less than a year, the company moved from near insolvency to a healthy, going concern. It was exhilarating."

Kim said, "Wow, why did you ever leave that place?"

"Unfortunately, once we hit profitability and the pressure was off, the old barriers snapped back into place. People returned to their corner offices and the cronyism, politics, and nasty behaviors returned with a vengeance. It was disgusting and demoralizing. I left soon after."

"Kind of like the 9/11 disaster," the nurse offered. "In the weeks following, this country pulled together and even members of congress gathered and sang God Bless America on the Capitol steps. Average Americans were genuinely kinder and more civil, and highway statistics showed that road rage decreased significantly. But it quickly passed."

The coach could relate. "So true, Kim. I think of natural disasters like an earthquake in San Francisco or Hurricane Katrina. People pull together, and it doesn't matter who is rich or poor, black or white, inner-city resident or suburb dweller. People work shoulder-to-shoulder to serve one another because survival is at stake.

"Unfortunately, those times of camaraderie and community are short-lived."

The teacher sighed. "Short-lived indeed. Even though community can be quickly formed in response to a crisis, it can collapse just as quickly once the emergency passes. People return to their suburbs, corner offices, and politics,

Chapter Nineteen: Functioning

and the personal barriers snap right back into place."

The light went on for the principal. "Since most of life is not a crisis, the group's real challenge is how do we build and sustain community in the absence of a crisis?"

The teacher smiled. "Bingo, Theresa.

"Which brings us to the final stage of group development, the functioning stage, when group members finally take personal responsibility for the success of the team. They are becoming aware of their personal barriers and are working to eliminate them. The group now begins to move toward community and synergy."

"Synergy? Definition, please," the principal predictably requested.

"Thought you'd never ask, Theresa! One plus one equals three or more. Synergy is the force multiplier that occurs when we work together rather than against each other."

The teacher raised his left hand. "It's like the fingers on my hand. Individually, they are not all that strong, but if I pull them together, they form a very powerful fist."

"What other dynamics occur in community?" the principal pressed.

"Not only do group members begin to work on their personal barriers, but they also begin practicing healthy behaviors like assertiveness and active listening skills. Character, excellence, and respect become the behavioral rules of the house.

"Paradoxically, once the bad behaviors get rooted out and people stop trying to fix and change one another, a lot of personal growth and change begins to occur naturally.

"High-performing team members often say they feel psychologically safe in the group. Safe to be themselves without fear of ridicule, condemnation, judgment, politics, or other destructive behaviors that destroy trust and relationships.

The Culture

"But high performance, community, is slippery. It's one thing to achieve community for a season and another thing to sustain it over time. Community requires commitment."

The sergeant wasn't sure. "Is this really possible? My skeptical meter is rising because it sounds a little too perfect."

The coach responded first. "Certainly not perfect, Greg, but far superior to the level where most teams operate. Coach Lombardi used to say, 'We will chase perfection, and we will chase it relentlessly, knowing all the while we can never attain it. But along the way, we shall catch excellence.'"

The teacher looked pleased. "Stage four is by no means perfect, and I do not want to imply that there is no conflict in community because there often is.

"But it is a different kind of conflict because group members have hope, excitement, and anticipation that a solid resolution will be hammered out because we are in it together. The group has learned to work and solve problems together gracefully without emotional bloodshed.

"Community is an arena where the players have learned to lay down their weapons, personal barriers, and have begun to practice new behavioral skills like listening, transparency, humility, assertiveness, and servant leadership. Emotional connections, bonding and a deeper trust develops, which is the 'secret sauce' to becoming a community."

"How do you know when you've reached community with a group, Simeon?" the principal asked.

The teacher paused. "People generally know when a group is operating at this level because community is palpable; you know something special is going on. Maybe that's where the term community spirit comes from.

"I'm curious. Have any of you ever experienced a high-performing team or true community?"

The coach had. "Throughout my years in coaching,

Chapter Nineteen: Functioning

I experienced community on three different occasions, and I will never forget the feeling of being 'in the zone' with those teams. We connected on so many levels and so intensely. To this day, many of us are still in contact."

The sergeant had as well. "On two deployments overseas, with two different units, we became so tight that we could finish each other's sentences. We would do anything for one another, including dying, which some did."

The principal was curious. "How does the group make decisions when working in community?"

The teacher winked. "Keep those great questions coming, Theresa. Group decisions are made by consensus."

The sergeant objected. "Not sure I agree with that one, Simeon. My paradigm is consensus is an excuse for doing things by committee and abdicating your leadership responsibility. But I may well be wrong on this, so please challenge my thinking, sir."

The teacher nodded. "To be honest, Greg, there was a time when I would have agreed with you.

"But after experiencing higher levels of community with some of my executive teams, I got to the point where I simply did not want to make key decisions without their input. Once I began to know them on deeper levels, I developed a profound respect for them as well as trust in their judgment. I began to truly believe that our collective wisdom was superior to something I could come up with by acting independently.

"Which may be why in our country we will not convict a defendant without a consensus of jurors. It takes longer and is tricky at times, but better decisions are made if the process is followed."

The sergeant didn't seem convinced. "What were the ground rules?"

"First, only important decisions were made by consensus

because it takes some time. Second, there was no voting. We all agreed and committed ourselves to be fully present and hammer out the best decision possible that we could all live with. This meant throwing everything on the table and fully showing our hands.

"But the most important ground rule was this: Whatever decision was made, each team member committed to fully support the decision. Even when—especially when—someone didn't agree with the decision. After all, everyone had the opportunity to understand the issues, weigh in, and be heard, as well as hear all the other points of view around the table.

"But once the play was called and we broke huddle, we all supported the play and did everything in our power to make the play successful."

"What if the play was a disaster?" the sergeant pushed.

"That happened a lot. We would then re-huddle and work out a new play based upon the new data. But we only argued or disagreed about the play in the huddle, never in front of the team. The leaders have to be aligned."

The sergeant pushed further. "But what if the group could not reach consensus? What if even one person on your team could not agree? What happened then?"

"I made the call."

"You dictator, you," I teased.

The teacher laughed heartily.

"Seriously, Simeon, why did you get to make the call?" the nurse asked.

"Two reasons, Kim. First, somebody had to make the call because the world continued to move on and action needed to be taken.

"And second, I had the greatest risk. As CEO, if things fell apart, the board would be looking for my head."

The sergeant was coming around. "I like that. If

Chapter Nineteen: Functioning

consensus cannot be reached, the highest-ranking person in the room makes the final call. Is that correct?"

"Yes, and it rarely happened. Because if I chose to overrule the team, I knew in my heart that I had to be missing something. That was the kind of respect I had for my teammates and the community we had built.

"As a word of caution, only groups who have evolved through the stages and have worked on their barriers together are mature enough to problem-solve by consensus. Sadly, that eliminates most groups."

"Very sad," the nurse said quietly. "Culture is a huge competitive advantage for any organization. Why don't all organizations grow their leaders and build community?"

I knew the answer. "Ignorance and laziness, Kim. Ignorance because these principles are rarely taught in the corporate world. And laziness because growing leaders and building community require a great deal of commitment and a huge amount of effort. Let's face it, this stuff is hard. Dictatorship or just plain abdicating your responsibility as a leader to create excellence is so much easier.

"And many, myself included, choose the easier path."

During our late afternoon break, I decided to seek counsel from the teacher.

I searched and found him sitting on a bench, facing the lake and feeding the birds. I sat down beside him, trying unsuccessfully to avoid the droppings.

The teacher looked intently into my eyes. "What is it, John?"

I quickly confessed. "As you've probably gathered, things aren't going so well in my life. My marriage. With my kids. At work."

"I'm sorry," Simeon sighed as tears welled up in his eyes. The Teacher was a living example of human empathy, a skill I was only beginning to understand.

"I'm doing my part, Simeon. We talked here about taking responsibility, and I am doing that. I bring home the bacon, come home sober most of the time, avoid having affairs, and try to be there for the kids. I mean, I am doing my part, but she's got to meet me halfway. After all, marriage is 50/50."

The teacher laughed. "The genius who said marriage is 50/50 probably wasn't married very long. Divorce is 50/50. Marriage is 100/100. A great marriage, like any great organization, is a group of all leaders taking responsibility for the success of the team. Everyone is all-in."

Simeon paused before hitting me hard.

"Are you all-in, John?"

Chapter Twenty

GROWING LEADERS

*Failure is not fatal,
but failure to change might be.*

Coach John Wooden

Following the break, the coach was agitated.

"Okay, gang. We've spent a lot of time kicking around *what* needs to be done. It's time to get to the *how*.

"I mean I get it. Effective leaders must create a culture of excellence by growing leaders, including themselves, and building community. Got it. Agree with it. Awesome.

"But how do we turn these thoughts into realities? As Kim mentioned earlier, we spent several days talking at our retreat two years ago, yet only Greg was able to achieve real and sustainable changes in his life."

The coach turned toward the sergeant.

"Greg, I don't want you to take this the wrong way, but two years ago, I experienced you as a clueless, arrogant drill sergeant on steroids. I certainly did not imagine you to be a teachable

The Culture

human being. To be frank, I thought you were a bully."

"Why, thank you, ma'am," the sergeant teased with a wink.

"Seriously, Greg, you have changed. A lot. And for the better. Would you mind explaining how that happened?"

The sergeant hesitated as though unsure of how to proceed.

"I have to admit, I nearly bailed on our retreat two years ago, convinced that this servant leadership jazz was crap, and tht all you people needed was a few weeks of boot camp with me so I could get your thinking straight for you.

"But Simeon said something that gave me pause. He challenged us with a simple, yet practical, question that kept me awake at night following that retreat. He asked, 'Is your leadership working for you?'

"To find our answer, Simeon suggested we look at the people we were leading and influencing at work and at home to decide whether good fruit was being produced. Were people thriving as a result of our leadership? Were we leaving people better off than when we found them?"

The teacher was nodding. "In the end, that is the test."

"Indeed it is, sir. So, I took you up on the challenge and did an honest personal inventory. Long story short, I didn't like what I saw."

Greg addressed the coach. "And you are correct, young lady. I was clueless, but actually, it was even worse. I was militantly ignorant, which as I said earlier, is what you think you know but don't know. I knew about leadership but didn't know leadership at all."

"So what did you do about it, Greg?" I asked, aching for answers.

"Three simple things, John. One, I collected some data. Two, I took responsibility and owned it. Three, I did something about it."

"More specifics, please?" the principal inquired.

"I decided I needed to collect data points to identify the gaps between the high standard of servant leadership and my performance. To do this, I intuitively knew I needed to get straight, honest feedback from the people I was leading.

"That was tough for me. Sucking it up and asking for honest feedback was humbling. And as you all remember, humility was not my strong suit.

"I started with my wife and questioned her about our marriage, including what she needed versus what she was getting from me. I did the same thing with the kids. It took awhile to get them talking, but once they did, a lot of angry stuff came pouring out. At first, I got mad and pouted a bit, probably to cover up how crushed I felt.

"But I didn't stop. Back at the base, I scheduled meetings with several peers, a couple of supervisors as well as numerous subordinates, to solicit their candid feedback. I even requested a confidential 360-degree assessment from one of the platoons I was leading.

"As you can probably guess, the results were rough, though humiliating might be the most accurate word. I initially went into denial, which soon morphed into anger as I tried to justify things in my head. Finally, I descended into a brief period of depression."

The nurse jumped in. "Greg, your experience sounds like the emotional stages of death and dying that Elisabeth Kübler-Ross wrote about in her classic book."

"I don't know about all of that, Kim, but what I do know is that it took me a few weeks before I could accept it and own it. And once I owned it, I made the choice to do something about it. But getting to that point was painful."

Theresa, our group quote-Nazi, was ready. "The late *7 Habits* author, Stephen Covey, used to say that few people have the humility to change without some pain."

The nurse nodded. "Pain can be a good thing when it creates the necessary friction to get us moving toward change. Pain gets us to the doctor, dentist, marriage counselor, AA, church, and other helpful places as we seek relief. Places we might not have considered were it not for the distress we are experiencing."

I needed more. "So what did you do next, Greg?"

"I put together some specific and measurable behavioral action plans. I enlisted accountability partners, including my wife, son, boss, a couple of peers and key subordinates, and I checked in regularly with them for feedback on how they thought I was doing. I also did some follow-up 360-degree work to determine if I was closing the gaps between where I needed to be and where I was.

"It didn't happen overnight, but gradually, I began to grow and improve."

The teacher provided clarity. "Growing as a leader, which is essentially improving our character, boils down to a three-step process."

"Please keep it simple, Simeon," the principal cautioned. "Albert Einstein said if you can't explain it simply, you don't understand it well enough."

"Simplicity is one of my favorite words," the teacher assured her as he moved to an empty whiteboard.

Growing Leaders

1) Foundation (Set the Standard)
   Continuous Learning
2) Feedback (Identify the Gaps)
   Continuous Input/Data
3) Friction (Eliminate the Gaps)
   Continuous Improvement

Chapter Twenty: Growing Leaders

The coach looked proud. "We are back to my Three F's."

The teacher winked. "We are indeed, Chris. It's a great model for any change process.

"The first step is setting the standard and getting intellectual understanding and agreement of what excellence in leadership looks like.

"This education and training must be consistent and ongoing because continuous learning—repetition—is the mother of learning. Reading a book or attending a seminar will not suffice. You cannot hear these principles once and think you've got them locked in. We need to be reminded often."

The preacher couldn't resist. "You know the old saying—there's a reason why church is every Sunday."

"Obviously, training is not enough," the coach exclaimed. "Otherwise, more than one of us would have made sustainable changes following our first retreat."

"Exactly, Chris," the teacher affirmed. "Continuous learning is an important first step in growing leaders but much more is required."

I felt like a human sponge as I furiously took notes. "Keep going, Simeon," I encouraged.

"The second step is the feedback portion, or identifying the gaps between where we currently are versus where we need to be as leaders. This involves fleshing out our gaps or our 'stuff,' and we all have stuff."

The principal was giggling. "Yeah, if you don't think you have stuff, that makes more stuff."

I added, "And if you still don't think you have stuff, just ask the folks around you. They'll be happy to give you plenty of feedback about your stuff!"

The teacher laughed. "There is a great leadership feedback tool I have used over the years that I will email to

141

The Culture

you if you wish.[4] I believe it asks the right questions against the high standard of leadership we have been discussing. It is also a great tool for identifying our personal barriers.

"Getting good feedback is crucial. Do not assume that you have a good handle on your stuff. My experience is that many people are clueless about their gaps. That doesn't mean they're bad people; they've just never had any honest feedback.

"Which brings us to the third step, which is creating friction. A healthy level of friction, or tension if you prefer, is essential in getting people serious about change, continuous improvement, and getting after their stuff."

"I don't like friction or pain," the nurse moaned. "But it can definitely get us moving in the right direction. How did you create this necessary friction, Simeon?"

"With my teams, each member would pick two areas of opportunity based on the feedback they received. They would write a minimum of two specific and measurable action plans detailing what they were going to do to grow and close their gaps."

I was skeptical. "And that was enough friction to get them to change?"

"Heavens no, John. That was only the beginning. We would then meet as a team and openly discuss our feedback scores with one another and share our specific action plans going forward. Greg earlier called this 'opening-the-kimono,' and it is a powerful exercise.

"In addition, the team would meet regularly to report on individual progress. There was simply nowhere to hide because everyone was watching.

"Anything else?" I asked, feeling a little nervous.

---

[4] This tool can be found in Appendix B.

"Each leader would then meet with their individual teams and openly share their feedback results along with specific action plans for changing and growing as their leader. Follow up meetings throughout the year were also scheduled."

I was taken aback. "Wow, that's pretty much in your face. Once you've spilled the beans in front of everyone, there's nowhere to hide. I don't know if I could be that transparent and humble."

The sergeant laughed. "But here's the thing, John. You're not telling them anything they don't already know. They are the ones who gave you the feedback, remember? They spend half their waking hours working with you. They already know your stuff."

"Good point," I conceded. "And maybe transparency and candor is good because we're left with a choice. We will either get serious about growing and getting after our stuff or we will get so uncomfortable that we may have to leave."

"That's right, John," the teacher concurred. "Sometimes there are casualties in the process of growing leaders as some people have been hiding a long time and just cannot take that much light shining into their world.

"I also want to mention an unexpected collateral benefit that always accompanies this process. Obviously, these sessions require team members to practice and develop the skills of transparency, vulnerability, and humility while simultaneously creating accountability to grow and improve. These dynamics enable the team to dive deeper together, which further strengthens the team's community."

The nurse was excited. "How cool is that. So efficient. And as you said, Simeon, you don't develop humility, grow your character, or build community by reading books or watching PowerPoint slides. You've got to practice this stuff."

"Exactly, Kim. To summarize, my years of experience have proven to me that the difficult part of growing leaders is not getting people to agree to the principles of servant leadership. As we have seen, the principles are self-evident. Everyone agrees.

"The difficult part is getting people to change. Foundation, feedback, friction. It might not be what people want, but it is certainly what people need. And servant leaders meet needs.

"We must help our people move the knowledge from their head into their hearts, and from their hearts into their habits. If we don't get these principles into our game, it's just information and of little value."

I couldn't resist.

"Intention minus action equals squat. Right, Simeon?"

"Precisely, my friend."

Chapter Twenty-One

BUILDING COMMUNITY

*Wearing the same shirts
don't make us a team.*

Factory worker

I was pumped.

The three F's were clear and simple; an achievable process just waiting to be executed.

"I can do this," I declared out loud, turning a few heads.

The coach wanted more. "Okay. We create a culture of excellence by growing leaders and building community. Check. We grow leaders by executing the three F's. Check.

"How do we build a high-performing team or community?"

The teacher grabbed the last remaining whiteboard and quickly wrote:

Building Community

1) Set the Rules of the House
2) Monitor/Enforce the Rules of the House
3) Develop Trust/Emotional Connections

The sergeant suddenly shouted, "Hooah to that, sir!"

The principal jumped in her chair. "Really, Greg? Hooah? What on earth is that about?"

"Sorry to startle you, ma'am. Hooah is an old military expression meaning heard, understood, and acknowledged. I got a little excited because number one is dead on.

"The leader must first ante up with expected team behavior. As was pointed out earlier, when people join a group, they have two subconscious questions: 'How am I supposed to behave, and what happens if I don't?' As the coach said earlier, you can't write speeding tickets if the speed limit signs aren't clearly posted."

The teacher smiled. "Precisely, Greg. Setting performance and behavioral standards creates expectations, sets boundaries, and ensures emotional and psychological safety—all crucial in creating a culture of excellence. Simply put, you must drive out bad behavior.

"It is crucial that the rules of the house be clear and simple. Here is what I suggest."

The teacher wrote:

Rules of the House

Character: <u>Do</u> the Right Thing
Excellence: <u>Do</u> Your Very Best
Respect: <u>Do</u> the Golden Rule

The teacher explained. "My experience has been that most everything that happens in an organization can be captured within these three guidelines, what I refer to as the three D's. Its genius lies in establishing the moral high ground while maintaining simplicity for all to understand and recall. What do you think?"

The group chewed on it for a while.

I was first to answer. "Character, excellence, and respect. I mean, how do you argue with that?"

The teacher continued. "In addition, three corollary coaching questions arise naturally from these guidelines.

What was the right thing to do?

Was that the best you were capable of doing?

Would you want to be treated the same way if the situation were reversed?"

"Love it," the coach said. "And their answers to the three questions become your coaching opportunities.

"What was the right thing to do? If they didn't know the right thing to do in a given situation, coach and counsel them. Was it the best they were capable of doing? If not, discuss what excellence looks like and assist them in acquiring the skills they lack . Would they want to be treated that way if the roles were reversed? If not, teach them, grow them, and serve them. And the questions reinforce our values."

The principal was equally excited. "It's awesome! If my students and faculty know that character, excellence, and respect are the standard, and they know the three questions I will be asking when performance or behavioral gaps arise, they will come to my office prepared to answer them. I can see how day-to-day decisions filtered through this prism will quickly morph into better choices and behaviors. And before long, these behaviors become the culture of the organization."

The teacher had more. "The reason I believe that these three guidelines and corollary questions are so powerful is that they answer three universal questions everyone has of one another:

Can I trust you?

Are you committed?

Do you care about me?'

"When we do the right thing, when we do our best, when we treat people the way we want to be treated, we answer each question with a resounding, Yes!"

The sergeant got pragmatic. "Listen, if someone cannot buy into the values of character, excellence, and respect, do you really want them on your team? My experience is that people who practice excellence do not work well with people who practice mediocrity. That is why leaders must be relentless in holding people accountable to the rules of the house. As we discussed, dumbing down the standards destroys morale and creates a culture of mediocrity."

The coach pushed us forward. "Simeon, why is the second step of building community about monitoring and enforcing the rules of the house? It seems obvious, even redundant, to the first step."

The principal hopped in. "Because a rule not enforced is no rule at all."

"Bingo!" the sergeant said. "Most organizations print endless mission statements, boast about their corporate values, and dazzle with never-ending clichés on their websites. But in the end, all that matters is how people actually behave."

The principal once again demanded clarity. "So what specifically do you mean by monitoring and enforcing the rules of the house, Simeon?"

The teacher did not mince words. "A total commitment to identifying and eliminating behaviors contrary to the rules of the house."

"Sounds tough," the principal said. "Examples?"

Chapter Twenty-One: Building Community

The teacher was ready. "Let me give you four scenarios to illustrate.

"You have a team member who achieves performance results and exhibits character and the right values. How do you respond?"

"Easy," the nurse blurted out. "We love you and want to clone you."

The teacher laughed. "That was a softball, Kim. Now, let's say you have someone who is not achieving results and also displays the wrong values. How do you respond?"

The nurse played along. "Easy. We love you, and we'll miss you."

"Another softball. Now, what about a team member who is not achieving performance results but has solid values and character?"

The nurse looked stumped, so I jumped in. "That's a little tougher. I would probably continue to work with them with the understanding that they had to get their results up fast."

"I would agree, John. Their good behavior earns them another chance, but the results must improve.

"Now suppose you have a team member who hits their numbers and gets results but displays poor values and character. They are duplicitous: kissing up to bosses, kick down to employees, even belittling customers behind their backs. In short, they display behaviors contrary to the rules of the house, and yet they hit and even exceed performance targets. How will you respond?"

I answered honestly. "Most managers, including me, would probably do little or nothing. I might secretly hope things improve, but getting results pretty much trumps everything else."

The sergeant looked disappointed in me. "But the message you just sent to everyone in the organization is that your values and culture are a joke.

"The right thing to do is cut them loose and announce to the team that although their numbers were good, they did not practice the values of the organization. Nothing sends a more powerful message than what you actually do. Values not monitored and enforced are no values at all."

"So what's the right thing to do, Kim?" the teacher challenged. "Remember, true leaders always do the right thing."

"Share them with the competition!" the nurse exclaimed, eliciting laughter from the group.

The coach stayed on point. "Okay, the last step of developing bonds and emotional connections. What's that about, Simeon?"

"During my career, at work or at home, I regularly set aside time for personal sharing and life stories, as well as other relational exercises. These exercises helped people bond and connect emotionally in deeper ways. I cannot overstate how transformational this is to any group."

"Examples, please," the principal requested.

"In meetings at work or around the dinner table at home, I would take a few minutes to ask the group probing questions like, 'What is the toughest thing you're going through right now?' or 'What is going really well in your life right now?' or 'What is the hardest thing you ever had to do?' or 'What is the most important lesson you've learned in life?' The list of possible questions is endless.

"In addition, I looked for opportunities to conduct periodic off-site activities like group outings, experiential exercises, charitable work in the local community, et cetera.

"Predictably, as the group begins to feel psychologically safe and emotionally connected, relationships deepen and the fruit appears in the form of trust, commitment, excellence, and community."

The preacher looked excited. "I just had an insight.

Chapter Twenty-One: Building Community

Growing leaders helps to build community, and building community helps to grow leaders. Let me see if I can explain this thought.

"As Simeon has explained, growing leaders and building community are essentially about changing and developing new habits.

"I recently read a book about the power of habits, and research clearly shows that for a permanent change to occur, people must believe that it is possible for them to change.

"The data overwhelmingly shows that this belief comes primarily from a group experience. The book cited numerous examples, such as AA, weight reduction groups, smoking cessation programs, group therapy, and many others that have successfully helped people change and grow.

"Community, as we've described it, provides the essential ingredients for people to change and grow as leaders. It creates a safe environment where people can observe change and growth in others and come to believe it is possible for themselves. Community also provides the necessary support, encouragement, and accountability to make the new behaviors sustainable over time."

The teacher was impressed. "Fantastic insights, Lee, and as you said earlier, community on a team is a force multiplier. I will never understand why organizations fail to utilize the power of community. Can you imagine competing against a team operating at that level?"

The coach still needed more. "Okay, Simeon. Creating a culture of excellence requires growing leaders and building community, and we now have a roadmap for each. Check and check.

"But where do you find the time to do this stuff with all the other tasks that bombard us daily?"

"Great question, Chris, and the answer is deceptively simple. Not easy, but simple. You must commit two hours per month specifically to the process of growing leaders and building community."

Impulsively, I blurted out, "I'm not sure I have the time for that."

"Let's do the math, John. The average manager spends well over two-hundred hours per month on the job. Two hours per month equates to a mere one percent of the available working hours per month. You don't have one percent of your time to grow and sustain your culture?"

The sergeant piled on. "And let's not forget our premise from yesterday. Our competitive advantage is our people and our culture, while pretty much everything else is a commodity. If we cannot commit one percent of our time to create a culture of excellence by growing leaders and building community, then we simply do not believe our premise. Nor do we really believe anything else we talked about this weekend."

"A couple of hours per month is a big investment," I weakly countered, recognizing their faultless logic.

The teacher smiled. "I once had a frugal CFO ask me, 'What if we invest all this time and money in our people, and they choose to quit?' I countered with, 'What if we don't invest in our people, and they choose to stay?'"

I was running out of excuses.

The coach seemed intrigued. "So, what would this two hours per month look like?"

The teacher distributed a "Culture Meeting Agenda" as well as a "Group Guidelines" handout.[5]

"My teams would follow this simple agenda along with the group guidelines. Some groups met weekly for thirty minutes and others met bi-monthly for an hour. We would rotate the meeting facilitator for each meeting to reinforce the principle that we are a group of all leaders. It was never *my* meeting; it was *our* meeting."

---

5   See Appendices C and D for these handouts.

Chapter Twenty-One: Building Community

We spent a few minutes eyeballing the agenda.

The teacher continued. "As you can see, any junior high student could easily follow the agenda. We would simply rotate between growing leaders and building community.

"The available leadership and community-building topics are endless. For example, if you go to TED.com and do a leadership search, you will find hundreds of eighteen-minute teachings by some of the best leaders on the planet. Or just type 'community building exercises' into your search engine, and you will find enough to keep you busy well into the next century."

Silence again descended upon the group as we marinated in all we had learned.

After a few minutes, the clock chimed the late hour.

Our time together had come to an end.

Chapter Twenty-Two

EXECUTION

*What we think or what we believe is,
in the end, of little consequence.
The only thing of consequence is what we do.*

John Ruskin

With a few words, the teacher brought closure. "Our reunion has come to an end. Please know I have cherished our brief time together, and each of you has left your unique mark on me. I will miss you."

It was clear why Simeon was the rock star CEO of his generation. What a phenomenal leader.

Through personal sharing, humility, active listening, precise questioning, strategic interventions (as well as non-interventions), the teacher engaged, influenced, and inspired us. He captured the best from each of our unique life experiences, and we left knowing we had participated in something special. Something excellent.

The teacher left us better people than when we arrived. And, like the real pros often do, he made it look easy.

We said our final goodbyes, and as you might imagine, hugs and tears were flowing freely. A wave of emotion swept over me as I came to the realization that I loved these people.

Even the preacher.

Now I'm not saying that I will be spending my next family vacation with him, but I would be there in a heartbeat if he needed me. Maybe it was that emotional connection or community spirit thing we talked about.

Anyway, following the goodbyes, everyone scattered to gather their belongings before hitting the road. Alone in my room, I sat in the little rocking chair and thought deeply about the weekend, my life, and the personal changes I knew I had to make.

After some time, I headed out of the now-deserted building to take a final stroll around the beautiful grounds. Soon I came upon the teacher sitting on the same bench we had shared earlier. Our eyes met, and he gestured for me to sit.

We sat in silence, admiring the vast blue lake below, now covered in whitecaps from the steadily blowing westerly wind. The dry leaves were rustling and falling around us as the sun slowly made its way toward the distant horizon. The majesty and immense beauty of our surroundings was awe-inspiring and humbling.

Finally, I spoke. "You know, Simeon, maybe, just maybe, I'll get it right this time. But to be honest, I am scared stiff."

"Tell me why, John?"

"It feels like déjà vu. Two years ago, I was all pumped up like I am now, and yet I failed miserably."

Chapter Twenty-Two: Execution

The teacher clarified, "You experienced an outcome, not a failure."

I nodded, although I wasn't sure of the difference.

"Simeon, this time, I really have to change because I'm pretty sure this will be my last chance at home or even at work, for that matter."

"You have already changed, John."

"Do you really think so?"

"I do. Two years ago, you left here excited and self-assured—"

I interrupted. "You mean full of pride and arrogance."

"Perhaps, John. But much of that has been replaced with something quite beautiful."

"And what would that be?"

"Humility. You have become more authentic, vulnerable, other-focused, and teachable. Humility is the game-changer and the most important character skill a leader can develop."

"Why didn't you just tell me this two years ago and save me a lot of trouble?" I challenged, a bit put off.

"You weren't ready, John. You had to experience more, even suffer more, to grow more. You had to get to the end of yourself. There are no shortcuts."

I smiled. "When the student is ready, the teacher arrives."

The teacher looked deeply into my eyes. "Precisely, my friend."

My six-hour drive home became a solo and intense strategic planning session on executing change in my life.

Upon arrival, I assembled my wife, son, and daughter in the living room and matter-of-factly stated, "I have failed this family both as a husband and as a father."

The Culture

I copied the teacher's approach and allowed a minute or two of silence to let that settle in, which was tough for me. Tougher still was the involuntary stream of tears that began flowing down my face.

I continued. "I intend to make changes, big changes in my life and in our family. To do so, I will need help from each of you."

"Yeah, like what?" John Jr. asked with loads of attitude, his eyes never leaving the floor.

"Glad you asked, son. I will be spending time, a lot of time, with each of you, to get to really know you and understand how I can better meet your needs. I will need your honest and candid feedback so I can improve and grow. Can I count on you to help me?"

Dead silence. I joined my son in staring at the carpet.

After a couple of minutes, I slowly lifted my head to see if anyone was still in the room.

My wife's eyes were locked on me, and her mouth was hanging open. She looked to be in a state of shock.

John Jr. unfolded his defiantly clenched arms and slowly raised his head. He fixed his eyes directly on mine.

There must have been quite a snowball fight in Hell as my daughter, Sarah, actually laid her cell phone down and made eye contact with me for the first time in many months. Tears were streaming down her beautiful cheeks.

It appeared I had their attention.

When I returned to work the following morning, my personal mission became creating a culture of excellence. Which meant I had to get laser-focused on growing leaders and building community.

The first order of business was the usual 9:00 meeting

Chapter Twenty-Two: Execution

with my ten department managers. Check that, my ten department *leaders*.

As I surveyed the conference room table, I was saddened to observe all heads bowed down with eyes nervously glued to spreadsheets and notes, fearfully anticipating the usual interrogation, accusations, and bullying from me. My eyes watered as I reflected upon the culture I had created.

I took a deep breath and began.

"Good morning. I want to begin by making a confession to you all. I have failed you as your leader. I have failed to serve you properly by identifying and meeting your legitimate needs. I have failed to inspire and influence this team to excellence. I have created a toxic culture, and I am very sorry. I hope you will one day be able to forgive me."

I let that sink in with a full minute of silence before continuing

"But all of that is in the past. Beginning today, we are going to create a culture of excellence together. We will accomplish this by growing leaders, starting with me, and building a high-performing team together.

"We are going to become a group of all leaders, a community, who operate with character, excellence, and respect. I am also aware that none of this will happen without your help. Can I count on each of you?"

The bad news was I only got back a few grunts and polite nods. Who could blame them for being skeptical, even fearful.

The good news was their heads were now up and all eyes were focused in my direction.

I now needed to find the time in our busy work schedules to create and sustain our new culture of excellence.

The Culture

As we already had a standing weekly staff meeting, it seemed the logical place to begin. I looked through some of our old meeting agendas and quickly realized that a major portion of our meetings involved sharing operational metrics and updates. It dawned on me that all that information was easily accessible to any team member and was just silly corporate redundancy. No wonder our meetings were so boring.

By whacking the unnecessary stuff, I was able to find an hour every other week for our "Creating a Culture of Excellence" sessions. A few team members balked at the time commitment, but I stood my ground, pointing out that we could not call ourselves a culture-driven organization if we didn't take the time to practice growing leaders and building community. I said that would be like a football team saying they don't have time to practice blocking and tackling. You can call yourself whatever you want, but you're not a football team if you don't practice those things.

Following the teacher's agenda, we rotated the facilitator every meeting. The team utilized the Leadership Skills Inventory as we started to flesh out our gaps and personal barriers. My personal feedback was brutal, but that did not slow me down. To the contrary, it made me more determined than ever.

We then "opened our kimonos" with one another and began talking about our 'stuff,' beginning with me. We discussed what we were going to do to close our gaps, complete with specific action plans and corresponding metrics.

Within two weeks, I scheduled plant meetings, covering all three-hundred-plus employees on three shifts. In each meeting, I went over the new rules of the house and fielded questions.

I also had our maintenance team put up giant posters

Chapter Twenty-Two: Execution

throughout the plant with three simple statements:
Do What's Right (Character)
Do Your Best (Excellence)
Do the Golden Rule (Respect)

I was surprised at how receptive most people were to the idea. Oh, there were the usual naysayers, but their peers quickly quieted them down. After all, as the teacher said, I had the high moral ground with those three rules.

Transforming the posters into sustainable habits and culture would take some time, but that was okay with me.

I was all-in.

———◊◊◊———

Back at the ranch, I continued to work on building relationships and community. I scheduled several family outings as well as one-on-one time.

In addition, I began a new family tradition of dinners at 7:00 p.m. every weekday. Excused absences were only granted in the event of death or severe illness, accompanied by a note from the funeral director or doctor.

I also established a ten-minute ritual called "Question of the Day," immediately following dinner and while seated at the table. Each day, we would rotate who brought the question to the table, and the rule was that we all had to answer sincerely and honestly.

It was like pulling teeth the first few weeks, but soon the family began to look forward to the questions. Before long, if I forgot to do our "Question of the Day" after dinner, someone would quickly reprimand me.

I was amazed at what we learned about one another, the conversations generated, and how much fun we had utilizing this simple tool.

And more quickly than I could have imagined, our family dynamics began to change.

Back at work, the plant manager facilitated our first community-building exercise entitled 'My Life,' where each of the senior leaders spent ten minutes telling their life story from womb to tomb. I was pleased and amazed by the depth of the sharing. We learned things about one another that fundamentally changed the way we interacted.

In addition, the team did experiential exercises, Question of the Day, shared our ups and downs, and a host of other topics, depending upon what the facilitator brought to the table. We also did a ropes course and provided housing for a needy family in the community, along with other events and outings.

Our team soon began to know and experience one another on deeper levels. Emotional connections and bonds began to form, which morphed into trust.

The glue that holds it all together.

I was astonished at how quickly the fruit came.

AFTERWORD

Time marches on.
Over a year has passed since our reunion at St. John of the Cross, and you may be interested in a status report on my progress.

My answer?

I'm not where I need to be, but I'm better than I used to be.

Far better.

Green and growing.

How about you?

Appendix A

Common Personal Barriers to Relationships & Community

- Lack of Humility – Arrogance - Not Approachable or Teachable
- Talking Behind Other People's Backs (Backstabbing)
- Engaging in "Pairing" (Destructive Alliances Between People)
- Lacking Empathy/Compassion for Others
- Difficulty Being "Authentic" With Others
- Difficulty Handling Feedback or Constructive Criticism
- Dominating Discussions – Needs to be Smartest Person in the Room
- Insensitive to the Needs of Others - Self-Centered - Narcissistic
- Needing to be "Liked" By Everyone - Continually Seeking Approval
- Avoiding Conflict/Confrontation
- "Excluding" Self from Group (Emotionally/Physically)
- Over-Controlling/Micromanaging - Needing to Control Others
- Poor Listening Skills - Interrupting When Others Speak
- Lacking Commitment - Failing to Assume Appropriate Responsibility
- Having Preconceived Notions & Expectations
- Mood Swings - Unpredictable - Inconsistent
- Lack Of Patience & Self-Control – Losing Temper
- Publicly Embarrassing Others
- Prejudices - "Putting Other People into Boxes"
- Failing to Consider Contrary Thoughts & Opinions
- Failing to Be Honest – Deceptive - Not Trustworthy
- Failing to Be "Open" & Direct With Others - Hidden Agendas, etc.
- Failing to Be Respectful - Not Treating Others as Important
- Failing to Appreciate and/or Encourage Others
- Failing to Stand Up For Rights of Others or Self
- Failing to Voice "Contrary Opinion"
- Failing to Respect Confidentiality of Group/Others
- Failing to Forgive - Holding Resentments/Grudges

APPENDIX B

LEADERSHIP SKILLS INVENTORY

Leader's Name _____ Position _____ Department _____

	Strongly Agree	Agree	Disagree	Strongly Disagree
* Please check (✓) appropriate box - If you have no opinion about a particular statement, please leave the boxes blank				
01. Gives appreciation to others	❏	❏	❏	❏
02. Confronts people with problems/situations as they arise	❏	❏	❏	❏
03. Spends time walking floor & stays close to activity	❏	❏	❏	❏
04. Gives encouragement to others	❏	❏	❏	❏
05. Makes clear to subordinates what is expected on the job	❏	❏	❏	❏
06. Is a good listener	❏	❏	❏	❏
07. Coaches/counsels employees to ensure goal compliance	❏	❏	❏	❏
08. Treats people with respect (as important people)	❏	❏	❏	❏
09. Is actively involved in the development of subordinates	❏	❏	❏	❏
10. Holds people accountable for meeting the set standards	❏	❏	❏	❏
11. Gives the credit to those who deserve it	❏	❏	❏	❏
12. Shows patience and self-control with others	❏	❏	❏	❏
13. Is a leader people feel confident following	❏	❏	❏	❏
14. Has the technical skills necessary to do the job	❏	❏	❏	❏
15. Meets the legitimate *needs* (as opposed to *wants*)	❏	❏	❏	❏
16. Is able to forgive mistakes and not hold grudges	❏	❏	❏	❏
17. Is someone people can trust	❏	❏	❏	❏
18. Does *not* engage in backstabbing/duplicitous behavior	❏	❏	❏	❏
19. Gives positive feedback to subordinates when appropriate	❏	❏	❏	❏
20. Does *not* embarrass people or or punish them publicly	❏	❏	❏	❏
21. Sets high goals for self, subordinates, and department	❏	❏	❏	❏
22. Has a positive attitude on the job	❏	❏	❏	❏
23. Is sensitive to the implications of their decisions on others	❏	❏	❏	❏
24. Is a fair and consistent leader and leads by example	❏	❏	❏	❏
25. Is *not* an over-controlling or over domineering person	❏	❏	❏	❏
26. Displays humility is not arrogant, but authentic & approachable	❏	❏	❏	❏
27. Shows kindness & empathy toward others	❏	❏	❏	❏

What are the greatest Leadership strengths/skills that the person being evaluated possesses?
_____
_____

What Leadership skills does the person being evaluated need to work on and improve?
_____
_____

Appendix C

"Culture-Building Session" - Agenda

I. Start/End on Time - All Attend Unless Emergency/Death/Vacation!

II. Why Are We Meeting Today? (1 Minute)
- We agree that "the business of business is people"
- We agree that "our competitive advantage is our people"
- We agree that we must "Grow Leaders" & "Build Community"

III. "Culture-Building" Guidelines: Read a Section & Discuss (2 Minutes)

IV. Growing Leaders: (15–20 Minutes)
- Sharing Leadership Skills Inventory Results; SMART Action Plans & Progress
- Ted.com Leadership Clips (all 20 minutes or less/hundreds available online)
- Book Studies: *7 Habits*; *The Servant*; *The Culture*; *Good to Great*; others?
- Speakers from Corporate; Outside Organizations; Customers; Suppliers; etc.
- Business Journal Articles; Business Case Studies; etc.
- Other? (group brainstorming; other leadership development ideas)

V. Discussion: Weigh-In/Questions/Takeaways from Session? (10 Minutes)

VI. Building Community: (20 Minutes)
- "Community Building" Exercises (thousands available online)
- "My Life" Exercise; "One Thing" Exercise; "Barrel" Exercise
- "Open-the-Kimono" - "Question of the Day" Exercises
- "SWOT" Exercise (Strengths/Weaknesses/Opportunities/Threats)
- "Start/Stop/Continue" Exercise
- Other?

VII. Group Weigh-in (10 Minutes)
- What's going well/not well? How can we support you?

VIII. Next Session: Date? Time? Facilitator?
- Rotate Facilitator for each Meeting (A Group of all Leaders!)

IX. Session Ends on Time or Early - Email Minutes to Interested Parties

Appendix D

"Culture-Building Session" - Group Guidelines

I. Commitment
  A. Be a "Group of All Leaders" - Take Responsibility For Success/Safety of the Group
  B. Be Fully Prepared - Bring Excellence to Group
  C. Be Fully Present (Physically & Emotionally) – Participate & Engage
  D. Be Responsible to Keep Group on Point & on Task

II. Behavior
  A. Do Become Aware of Your Personal Barriers & Practice Setting Them Aside
  B. Do Resist the Temptation to Fix or Change Others
  C. Do Voice Feelings of Displeasure to the Group
  D. Do Avoid "Pairing", Pouting or Quitting; Work Out Concerns with Group

III. Communication - Speaking
  A. Speak Assertively – Open-Honest-Direct but Never Violate the Rights Of Others
  B. Speak in the 1st Person Using "I" Statements - ("I Think - I Believe - I Need")
  C. Speak Only When Moved to Speak (When in Doubt, Better to Remain Silent)
  D. Speak Personally & Deeply - Model Transparency & Humility

IV. Communication - Listening
  A. Do Actively Listen – Listen with an intent to understand rather than to reply
  B. Do Avoid Sidebar Conversations - One Person Speaks at a Time
  C. Do Not Interrupt When Others are Speaking - "Bracket" Your Thoughts
  D. Do Resist Urge to "Fill The Vacuum" With Your Words - Silence is Golden

Appendix E

Coaching: The 3 F's

1) Foundation – Set the Standard
   (What are the Expectations?)
2) Feedback - Identify the Gaps
   (Between Standard & Performance)
3) Friction – Coach the Gaps
   (Increase Positive & Eliminate Negative Gaps)

Rules of the House: The 3 D's
(& Corollary Questions)

1) Do the Right Thing - Character
   (Did you do the right thing?)
2) Do your Very Best - Excellence
   (Did you do your very best?)
3) Do the Golden Rule - Respect
   (Did you treat them as they should be treated?)

Constructive Discipline: The 3 E's

1) Establish the Gap
   (Between Standard & Performance)
2) Explore the Reasons for the Gap
   (Evaluate whether you have a discipline Problem)
3) Eliminate the Gap
   (Set Action Plans & Follow Up)

Appendix F

Growing Leaders

1) Foundation (Set the Standard)
   Continuous Learning
2) Feedback (Identify the Gaps)
   Continuous Input/Data
3) Friction (Eliminate the Gaps)
   Continuous Improvement

Leadership Defined

The skill of influencing people to action, with character that inspires confidence & excellence.

7 Leadership Principles

= Awesome Responsibility

= Skill

≠ Power (or Management)

= Authority (Influence)

= Serving

= Coaching

= Character

About the Author

In addition to *The Culture*, Jim Hunter is the author of two other internationally best-selling books: *The Servant: A Simple Story About the True Essence of Leadership* and *The World's Most Powerful Leadership Principle: How to Become a Servant Leader*.

His books serve as texts in many MBA and other higher-education curricula around the world, are translated into dozens of languages, and have sold well over five million copies worldwide.

Jim is a sought-after speaker to audiences around the world on leadership and developing high-performing teams. He also assists organizations in creating a culture of excellence by growing leaders and building community.

His clients include many of the world's most admired organizations including seven Malcolm Baldrige Quality Award Winners, *American Express*, *Johnson & Johnson*, *McDonald's*, *Nestlé*, *Procter & Gamble* and the *United States Army*, *Navy*, *Air Force*, and *Marine Corps*.

For more information, visit www.jameshunter.com.

Acknowledgments

To my awesome clients - For all you have taught me

To John Vella - For your insights, encouragement & friction

To my SNS family - For all we have experienced together

To my daughter, Rachael - For making my life so rich

To my bride, Denise - For being my best gift ever from Him